PRAISE FOR *THE BIG PUSH*

"This is a manual for taking us to the finishing line of gender equality. A jolt of new energy for longstanding feminists and a 'must read' for our new generations. Without understanding the incredible tentacles of patriarchy and its reinventions, we are destined to fight old battles as well as new ones. Cynthia Enloe, a great scholar and source of wisdom, pries open jammed patriarchal doors and nails the continuing reasons for gender inequality. A brilliant critique and a manifesto for our resistance."   — Helena Kennedy, QC

"Cynthia Enloe is, quite simply, brilliant. Her insight, her analysis and her clarity make *The Big Push* a must read for politicians, for staff of the UN, and it is just an absolute delight for those of us who thought we knew how power works, but needed to be reminded. Cynthia weaves it all into an intricate and recognisable web. I loved it."

—Madeleine Rees, Women's International
League for Peace and Freedom

"In what has clearly become a unique Cynthia Enloe lens and approach, *The Big Push* connects the dots in an engaging and original manner. It exposes the intricate and often invisible ways in which patriarchy survives and sustains itself. Yet, in a post-truth era in which populism, Brexit, Donald Trump, nationalist political parties and right-wing anti-immigration movements flourish, *The Big Push* also provides us with hope. Enloe leaves us in no doubt that feminist resistance is alive and kicking everywhere: intersectional transnational feminist analyses and activisms are locally and globally at the forefront of challenging patriarchy and its brothers: militarism, authoritarianism and neo-liberal economics."   —Nadje Al-Ali

"Cynthia Enloe mixes razor-sharp analysis of contemporary patriarchy with profound empathy for women's multiple forms of resistance. Without d[...]   [...]minist of our age."
—Melissa Benn

"Physics has unified field theory; feminism has Cynthia Enloe. In this fascinating book, she shows us the unifying thread that runs through so many systems: sugar production in Guyana; peacemaking efforts in Syria; domestic workers' conditions in Jamaica; tourism at Gettysburg; political protest in Washington, D.C. Examining masculinities and femininities to explore the ways patriarchy insinuates and propagates itself, she gives us powerful tools for understanding and change. And, with her usual alchemy, she makes an entertaining page-turner out of a serious subject."   —Sohaila Abdulali

"This really is such an important book. It's an accessible, incisive examination of the historical persistence of everyday patriarchy and how it plays out in today's international politics (and it's not all about Donald Trump)."   —Margaret Busby

"Cynthia Enloe is an adventurer, an intellectual with a light touch and inveterate 'feminist curiosity'; here she is again travelling across time and space – revisiting her own great history as an activist scholar, the landscapes of new and old wars, new and old political settlements, new and old trades in bananas and bombs; in all of them she shows how thinking about gender, the renewal of patriarchy and women's resistance, is vital to making sense of the world. It is a joy to travel with her."
                    —Beatrix Campbell

The Big Push

*Exposing and Challenging
the Persistence of Patriarchy*

Cynthia Enloe

First published in 2017 by

Myriad Editions
www.myriadeditions.com

Registered address:
Myriad Editions
New Internationalist, The Old Music Hall,
106–108 Cowley Rd, Oxford, OX4 1JE

First printing
1 3 5 7 9 10 8 6 4 2

A CIP catalogue record for this book
is available from the British Library

ISBN (pbk): 978-0-9955900-0-7
ISBN (ebk): 978-0-9955900-1-4

Typeset in Janson MT Pro
by WatchWord Editorial Services, London

Printed and bound in Great Britain
by Clays Ltd, St Ives plc

In memory of

Jean Hardisty (1945–2015)
Alison Bernstein (1947–2016)
Teresia Teaiwa (1968–2017)

Friends, teachers, feminists extraordinaire

CONTENTS

It's Not All About Trump

Confession: I almost broke into a run to get away from the first person I heard utter the word "patriarchy." We had been sitting at a picnic table on a lovely June afternoon. It was the lunch break at one of the early meetings on women and international development. It was all exciting; everyone was rethinking their experiences and trading new hunches. Then, over salads and drinks, someone said "patriarchy." I fled (well, I think I just said I was going for a refill of my iced tea).

Patriarchy. It sounded so heavy, so blunt, so ideological. I wasn't interested in ideology, at least not in employing it myself. Instead, I was interested in nuances, in gritty realities, in the mundane workings of everyday sexism as it crept into policy and actions.

I was wrong. Patriarchy does not blot out nuance. Patriarchy does not overlook the mundane. As I began to understand, the concept of patriarchy is not a club with which to batter complexity into simplicity. Quite the opposite. Patriarchy is a searchlight, a concept that can enable us to see what we otherwise might miss: the connective tissues between large and small, subtle and blatant forms of racialized sexism, gendered misogyny and masculinized privilege.

Donald Trump may be the latest gift to those who seek to perpetuate patriarchy. His celebrity, his bizarre tweets, his outlandish claims, yes, even his orange hair, together serve to capture our attention. Today, from Brighton to Boston to Beijing, one can say "Trump" and provoke an immediate reaction. He hogs the stage.

It is risky, I think, to become so diverted by the patriarchal machinations of any outsized figure that we shrink our curiosity about less attention-grabbing, more insidious dynamics that are perpetuating patriarchal ideas and relationships. Patriarchy existed before Donald Trump—and before the rise of the newest nationalistic, racist, misogynist political parties—and, unless we together reflect on its mundane causes, it is too likely to exist after Trump has retired to his golf club and the latest right-wing parties have been temporarily defeated.

It has been with this worry in mind that I have crafted this book. Trump does not loom large on these pages. Yet it is precisely my concern that preoccupation with any super-scale political figures will divert us from self-reflection and deep investigation that has provided the motivation for writing it.

It was Jana Lipman, Vernadette Gonzalez, and the beloved late Teresia Teaiwa who nudged me to think afresh about my mother's and my road trips to American battlefields, and Ruri Ito and her splendid Japanese feminist friends who made sure I thought seriously about what it meant to visit Hiroshima as a tourist. Ayşe Gül Altınay and Andrea Peto have kept me thinking anew about World War I narratives and especially Turkish women's understandings of that deadly conflict. Jef Huysmans and João Nogeira were so generous in their mappings of international sociology as to accept the smallest of gestures by military wives as fodder for theorizing. For inviting me to reflect on my ongoing journey toward feminist awareness, thanks go to Pauline Yu, Candace Frede, Susan Bailey and Philippa Levine of the American Council of Learned Societies. Each of the five chapters that had its start as a journal article has been significantly revised and reframed to speak to this book's core questions, but initially it took these encouraging editorial and scholarly colleagues to push each away from the dock.

Anne Marie Goetz, Nadine Puechguirbal, Madeleine Rees, Nela Porobić Isaković, Elin Liss, Cynthia Rothschild, Sanam Naraghi-Anderlini, Lena Ag, Laura Mitchell, Isabelle Geuskens, Mikaela Luttrell-Rowland, Carla Afonso, Adriana Benjumea, Christine Ahn, and all the activists in Women's International League for Peace and Freedom, individually and together, have tutored me on the deeply gendered workings of the United Nations. They have made me aware of the globalized feminist efforts to challenge tokenism and, instead, make "women, peace and security" meaningful in the lives of women coping with and resisting wartime violence and post-war patriarchy.

For the accounts featured in this book, I am indebted to the thoughtful gender-curious research and careful reporting of Sohaila Abdulali, Sanne Terlingen, Hannah Kooy, Xinhui Jiang, Beatrix Campbell, Melissa Benn, Ghazal Zulfiqar, Maya Eichler, Anita Fabos, Denise Bebbington, Kristen Williams, and Valerie Sperling. At the same time, critical scholars and friends Ken Booth and Toni Erskine nudged me to revisit the implications of Carmen Miranda for today's international politics.

No author thinks or writes in isolation. Friends ask fresh questions, lead one to new sources of reliable information, and keep one's spirits up in order to stay actively engaged in these dark times. Among the feminist friends who have specifically nourished this book project have been Gilda Bruckman, Serena

Hilsinger, Phi Pham, Laura Zimmerman, Margaret Bluman, Bob Benewick, Debbie Licorish, Amy Lang, Julie Abraham, Aleen Grabow, Lois Wasserspring, Annadis Rudolfsdottir, Sigga Ingadottir, Irma Erlingsdottir, and the members of the lively, politically savvy Sunday Afternoon Girlz Group and of our local feminist resistance huddle.

Iceland's celebrated artist Karolina Larusdottir (simply "Karolina" to her Icelandic admirers) is the creator of the wonderful print featured here on the cover. When I first saw Karolina's image, it made me laugh out loud. Those stolid, besuited patriarchal men clearly don't know what is happening to them. Karolina's title, *The Big Push*, inspired this book's own title. Julie Clayton and Ellen Sipple used their skills to create a digital version of *The Big Push*. I am grateful to Karolina Larusdottir's family and representatives for allowing me to use her art for the cover.

In these days of Trump, Brexit, and the upsurge of racist, misogynist right-wing parties, books, and newspapers—those things with pages that you can hold in your hands—are gaining new readers, and regaining readers who briefly imagined the internet was a sufficient source for staying informed as civic actors. It turns out that books have not gone the way of the dodo and the fax machine. Books—fiction and non-fiction—can be the source of complex analysis based on careful, transparent research; books can allow us to enter into multi-faceted lives quite unlike our own; books can be absorbed slowly, read and reread; books can be shared and provide sparks for surprising conversations.

It is thus with more appreciation than ever that I express my thanks to all the dedicated people who have used their skills to turn my laptop-tappings into the handsome book you are holding in your hands. Naomi Schneider, my longtime friend and editor, has been the insightful chief navigator of the book's acceptance and production by the University of California Press. At various steps along the way, the terrific Myriad production team has included Linda McQueen, Dawn Sackett, Louisa Pritchard, Isobel McLean, and Liron Gilenberg of Ironic Italics. At the helm of Myriad Editions is the superb feminist team of Candida Lacey and Corinne Pearlman; someday I'll reveal the role that Cuban *café con leche* played in our work together. For Candida and me, this project has had a special meaning, since Candida was editor for the very first edition of one of my earlier works, *Bananas, Beaches and Bases.*

It was my partner Joni Seager who gave me Karolina's print. It was with Joni that I laughed out loud at its wonderful image. It has been Joni with whom I have continued to investigate the twists and turns of modernizing patriarchy. Shared laughter, irreverence, energy, curiosity, companionship—that's what a sustainable feminist partnership looks like.

CHAPTER ONE

Pink Pussy Hats
vs. Patriarchy

The ground looks hard, with patches of snow under the tall northern trees. The salt-whitened rural road is empty of vehicles. Only a small band of walkers are heading toward an intersection, about a dozen people, some carrying posters, most wearing pink hats. It is January 21, 2017. This is the Women's March in the village (pop. 65) of Sandy Cove, Nova Scotia.[1]

A seventeen-hour drive west that same wintry Saturday would have brought one to Toronto's Women's March. There one would have joined a contingent of an estimated 50,000 Canadian marchers.[2] On January 21, a total of 34 towns and cities across Canada held Women's Marches. Crossing the border to travel further south (if one were not stopped by US border officials), one could have joined still-larger marches: Boston, 175,000; New York, 500,000; and, largest of all, Washington, D.C., with estimates of march participants ranging from 500,000 to 680,000.[3]

The Washington Women's March initially was sparked by Teresa Shook, a retired Hawaiian woman, who, in the wake of the presidential election, posted a Facebook call to friends, urging them to travel to Washington with her in January to protest the election's outcome. She later explained to reporters that she was just trying to take action as a way to absorb Donald Trump's Electoral College win of the 2016 presidential election, and Hillary Clinton's loss despite her victory in the popular vote.[4]

Teresa Shook was part of a complex relationship between American women voters, contemporary patriarchy, and the 2016 presidential election's gendered and racial dynamics. In each of the recent twenty-first-century American elections, slim majorities of white women had voted for the Republican presidential candidate. In this sense, 2016 followed an established pattern. Those white women who were most likely to vote for the Democrats' presidential candidate were single and/or college-educated: 51 percent of college-educated white women voted for Clinton. Yet four years earlier, in the 2012 presidential balloting, the Republican candidate, Mitt Romney, running against Barack Obama, won an even higher proportion of these white college-educated women's votes.[5]

According to exit polls conducted on November 11, 2016, 54 percent of all American women voters voted for Clinton. The pro-Clinton electoral majorities were especially high among women of color (94 percent of African American women voters, according to exit polls, chose to vote for Hillary Clinton, and 86 percent of Latina voters). While a slim majority of white women voters cast their ballots for Trump, only 41 percent of all men voted for Clinton. Again, the racial differences were stark, as majorities of men of color voted for Clinton.[6]

That means that, even if patriarchal presumptions, preferences, and prejudices had an influence on the 2016 presidential election, we will not be able to get to the bottom of how patriarchy plays out in a country's crucial electoral outcomes until we explore the inter-workings of gender, race, class, education, and marriage in the lives of women as voters (and non-voters) and men as voters (and non-voters).

"Women abandon Clinton" was a popular post-election claim. It was erroneous. A higher proportion of women of all major demographic categories voted for the 2016 Democratic nominee than had voted for male Democratic candidates in recently past presidential elections. That is, Donald Trump attracted a smaller proportion of women voters than had 2012 Republican presidential candidate Mitt Romney. This misleading portrayal of 2016's gendered dynamics, however, perpetuated two ideas that, if internalized by enough people, could serve to sustain contemporary American patriarchy. The first patriarchy-sustaining idea: there is no such thing as "American women," since American women are not only diverse, but also deeply fractured, even mutually hostile to each other. Patriarchy is always sustained by the "cat fight" cartoon version of women's relationships to each other. The second, and complementary, patriarchy-sustaining idea: most American women voters don't like/trust/respect/ approve of women as electoral candidates. In other words, the persistent marginalization of women in US political life is just fine with a majority of American women: most women are comfortable with the patriarchal system in which men run the country's political system.

The evolution of the Women's Marches of January 21, 2017, together with a fine-tooth-combed feminist investigation of 2016's actual voting patterns, belie both of these patriarchy-sustaining ideas.

Teresa Shook's modest Facebook post-election suggestion hit a common nerve. The Washington Women's March rapidly became a galvanizing event across the country and the world. It quickly outgrew Teresa Shook's own organizing capacities. The Washington Women's March's organizing baton was picked up by a quartet of young feminists, the majority of them women of color. By mid-January, that quartet grew to fourteen women. While none of the eventual organizing group had ever before organized such a rapidly evolving, multi-sited, large, and complex event, collectively they did possess what turned out to be the necessary toolkit of skills, perspectives, and experiences to make the Women's March and its multiplying "Sister Marches" a success: feminist intersectional analytical thinking, human rights advocacy experience, anti-racism organizing, fund-raising networks, alliance-building experience, Web design and merchandizing skills, and non-violent direct action training. They combined these with a shared conviction that the broadest mobilization would rise out of scores of grassroots initiatives. They were not obsessed with centralized control.[7]

Precisely because the Women's Marches were such decentralized, grassroots events, until the morning of January 21, the national organizers had little idea of how large the Washington March would become, or how many Sister Marches would be held across the country and around the globe. In Anchorage, Alaska, 3,500 women and men braved the cold to take part in their own local Women's March.[8] In Albuquerque, New Mexico, there were an estimated 15,000 marchers; in Birmingham, Alabama, 1,000; in Black Mountain, North Carolina, 400; in Charleston, West Virginia, 3,000; in Madison, Wisconsin, 100,000; in Sioux Falls, South Dakota, 3,300; and on the Midway Atoll (still an American colony in the Pacific) six people gathered to hold their own Women's March.

That is, Women's Marches were locally organized and boisterously attended not only in places often stereotyped as "Clinton territory." They also were held in regions whose residents have often been sweepingly characterized as stubbornly conservative in their views on the intertwined questions of gender and race. The very geography of the January 21 Women's Marches should make us more curious about the dynamic interplay of American racist sexism, on the one hand, and, on the other, regional cultures of voting and political activism. Sustaining American patriarchy turns out to be not a simple matter in regions away from the coasts.

It also was impossible to accurately forecast how many women and men outside the United States would see the rise of Donald Trump and of what might be called "trumpism"—a distinctive cluster of fears and aspirations propelling his political ascendancy—as engaging them in public expressions of resistance. The scores of Sister Marches that that engagement did inspire, from Antarctica to Fiji, took many observers by surprise. When reading the full list of 673 Women's Marches (with an estimated 4.9 million marchers), it helps to have an atlas at one's elbow.[9] Some marches were large, some tiny. For instance, according to preliminary estimates of the number of marchers:[10]

- Accra, Ghana—28
- Auckland, New Zealand—2,000
- Beijing, China—50
- Bristol, UK—1,000
- Calgary, Canada—5,000
- Cape Town, South Africa—700
- Dublin, Ireland—6,000
- Erbil, Iraq—8
- Gdansk, Poland—40
- Ho Chi Minh City, Vietnam—24
- Isle of Eigg, UK—30
- London, UK—100,000
- Melbourne, Australia—10,000

Of course, one wants to know what exactly motivated each woman, each man (the marches drew both, as well as those who defied sexual binaries) to make the effort to come out on that Saturday in January 2017 to be seen and heard. The overarching commitments appeared to be for women's rights, for racial and ethnic inclusivity, and for transparent democratic processes. Yet each person who chose to take part had a personal motivating analysis. Reading the list of Sister Marches also prompts one to explore what feelings and understandings—perhaps quite new— about themselves in this world each marcher carried home with them from each event.

In some places, it required taking a personal risk to participate in such a public political demonstration.

The Sister Marches list goes on:[11]

- Cairo, Egypt—4
- Manchester, UK—2,000
- Moscow, Russia—7
- Nairobi, Kenya—1,000
- Oaxaca, Mexico—3,000
- Phnom Penh, Cambodia—71
- Paris, France—12,000
- Reykjavik, Iceland—400
- Seoul, South Korea—2,000
- Stockholm, Sweden—4,000
- Tel Aviv, Israel—500
- Tokyo, Japan—648
- Whitehorse, Yukon, Canada—300

The American women organizers published a list of the Washington Women's March principles and commitments—for women's rights, against violence, against racism (institutional, political, and individual), for transgender rights, for reproductive rights, for affordable health care, for policies to address the causes and consequences of climate change.[12] One of the chief hallmarks of the marches, nonetheless, was the personal spontaneity and creativity that local participation inspired. The symbol of that was the "pussy hat." The hat was a hand-knitted (usually by the wearer or someone the wearer personally knew) cap made of pink or magenta yarn. It was square in shape, and, when donned, two of its corners popped up to resemble cat's ears. The message was feminist. "Pussy" was the crude term that Donald Trump had been caught on tape using in the company of other men while boasting of his sexual access to women, even when women attempted to reject his advances. The pink pussy hats were knitted and worn in irreverent defiance of that misogyny.

What became a global feminist knitting movement began when Krista Suh, a 29-year-old screenwriter in Los Angeles, started wondering how she could stay warm while walking in a march in Washington, DC in January. Then she asked herself: "How can I visually show someone what's going on?" She posed the question to her local knitters group at LA's Little Knittery. Together they created a simple knitting pattern in a vibrant color that would send a collective feminist message. To spread the word and keep their project grassroots in practice, they posted their simple pattern on Facebook and on global knitters' websites. It went viral.[13]

The intersectional analysis underpinning the Women's Marches suggested how far transnational feminist thinking had developed during the past four decades. Again, that thinking was expressed in spontaneous chanting and an array of home-made poster messages. Among the chants shouted by many marchers joyfully in unison:

"My Body, My Rights! My Body, My Rights!"

"Black Lives Matter! Black Lives Matter!"

"No Hate. No Fear. Immigrants Are Welcome Here!"

During the massive Washington march, hundreds of thousands of women and men—racially and ethnically diverse, old and young (scores of mothers and daughters), those new to demonstration politics and veterans of Second Wave feminist activism, ambulatory and in wheelchairs—announced themselves as having come to the capital from every state in the union. They walked shoulder to shoulder along Pennsylvania Avenue (where, only twenty-four hours earlier, the smaller, official Inauguration parade had occurred). A call-and-response chant was taken up:

"Tell Me What Democracy Looks Like!"

"This Is What Democracy Looks Like!"

The signs women and men in the numerous marches carried (no poles or sticks allowed) were drawn in myriad colors and scripts. In Boston, one woman held her hand-painted sign over her head: "Indigenous Women Exist-Resist-Rise!" Next to her another woman displayed her own sign: "There WILL Be a Woman President!" At the same time, down in Washington, a pink-hatted woman wore her sign strapped to her back: "If You Are Not Outraged, You Are Not Paying Attention." A middle-aged woman climbed atop a piece of street-cleaning equipment to display her sign: "Don't Call Us Radicals. We Are Informed Citizens." Another Washington marcher held a cardboard sign inspired by Eleanor Roosevelt: "A Woman Is Like a Tea-bag—You Can't Tell How Strong She Is Until You Put Her in Hot Water."

Several women in various cities came to their local Women's March dressed as early 1900s Suffragettes, wearing green, white and purple sashes that read "Votes for Women."[14]

The Canadian writer Margaret Atwood reported receiving multiple messages from marchers accompanied by photos, showing signs that were inspired by her best-selling dystopian novel,

The Handmaid's Tale, which told of a dark future in which a totalitarian state would take control of women's bodies. One marcher's sign declared: "Make Margaret Atwood Fiction Again!"[15]

Among the Washington March participants were feminists from other countries reporting back home what they were seeing. For example, Chinese feminist observers were there as journalists and translators to let their activist colleagues in China know what was transpiring. They said that this reporting was especially necessary because Chinese conservatives deliberately mistranslated and misrepresented the Women's March in order to discredit its principles and goals.[16] For instance, one Chinese graduate student was there, she said, to send translations of signs and chants back home to her Chinese feminist colleagues: to feel the energy of the marchers, and also to ensure that sexist Chinese reporters and Tweeters did not succeed in distorting the portrayal of the march.[17]

In keeping with the transnational and open spirit of the January events, women's Sister Marches around the world brought marchers' global messages together with local concerns. While many marchers expressed anger and alarm at Donald Trump's election, they also were propelled by the intersection of their own local feminist concerns with those seemingly becoming entrenched in the United States. For instance, Lepa Mladjenović, one of the co-founders of the feminist anti-militarism group Belgrade Women in Black, noted that the January 21st Belgrade Women's March was led by five women who came to the capital from small Serbian towns to hold a broad purple banner that spelled out in bold white letters: "*Ženski Marš Protiv Fašizma*": "Women's March Against Fascism." While "fascism" is a term used only sparingly among American feminist activists, it has deeper and sharper resonance among many European feminists, connoting as it does the distinctive package of authoritarian rule, racism, militarism, and contempt for women's physical, intellectual and political autonomy. In the minds of the Belgrade Women's March participants, trumpist ideas were fascist ideas, and those ideas were already, even before Donald Trump's presidency, gaining prominence in Serbia and other regions of the former Yugoslavia.[18]

Any movement that sparks widespread participation in diverse societies occurs in the midst not only of global conversations and mobilizations, but also at particular times in the ongoing evolution of local political worries, debates, and actions. In Dublin, the January 2017 Women's March occurred during the throes of a national campaign to repeal the Irish constitution's eighth amendment, the clause prohibiting abortions. Consequently, according to the prominent Irish feminist Ailbhe Smyth, the Dublin Women's March, while consciously part of a "worldwide resistance" and in "solidarity" with American feminists, featured among its diverse posters a long green and blue banner carried by seven women and one man. It read: "Coalition to Repeal the Eighth."[19]

In Stockholm, as already listed above, the Women's March drew an estimated 4,000 participants. Among them was Elin Liss, a feminist activist in the Swedish branch of the transnational anti-militarist Women's International League for Peace and Freedom (WILPF; ikff, in Swedish).[20] Just seven months earlier, Swedish feminists from many local groups had joined together with an array of Swedish human rights organizations to meet in the southern city of Malmö. Their agenda: to discuss the rights and needs of newcomers to Sweden, many of them fleeing war zones in Iraq, Syria, Somalia, Sudan, and Afghanistan. Sweden was on a journey to becoming a multi-racial, culturally diverse society. The path was proving rocky. The country also had a minister of foreign affairs, Margot Wallström, who for the first time declared (in 2015) that Sweden would pursue a "feminist foreign policy." Wallström explained that a feminist foreign policy was one which prioritized the fostering of women's and girls' rights, which implemented its national commitment to human rights everywhere, and which prioritized diplomacy over military responses.[21] Swedish feminists such as Liss were heartened, seeing Wallström's announcement as confirming what so many of them had been working toward for decades, both at home and internationally. By contrast, those Swedes who had stakes in Sweden's arms export companies, such as Saab, the maker not only of automobiles but also of jet fighter planes, voiced alarm. Sweden is not one of the world's top ten arms exporters, but arms exports to countries such as Saudi Arabia have played a significant role in Swedish economic growth.[22] On January 21, consequently, Stockholm's marchers voiced their belief in an intersectional form of transnational feminism, one that combined opposition to Trump's political agenda with support for global abortion rights and climate change prevention, coupled with voicing resistance to Sweden's rapidly rising anti-immigrant nationalist party, the Sweden Democrats.[23]

The January 2017 marches were thus not just the culmination of multiple US electoral campaigns; they came in the middle of other countries' electoral campaigns. On many marchers' minds was the rise of local nationalist parties, most of whose leaders wove the fear of foreign men as rapists and the defense of what they imagined to be the traditional patriarchal family into the fabric of their anti-immigrant, anti-refugee campaigns. As French marchers cast a wary eye on the anti-immigrant Front National, whose leader, Marine Le Pen, was one of the two contenders for France's presidency in the final run-off election in May 2017, next door many German Women's March participants were thinking ahead to their own country's upcoming elections in September

2017. Their marches expressed concern about the increasing popularity of their own anti-immigrant, pro-natalist nationalist right-wing party, Alternative for Germany. With the iconic Brandenburg Gate in the background, many Berlin marchers held up signs picturing Hitler next to Donald Trump. Others carried signs portraying a woman wearing a hijab decorated in red, white, and blue, with the caption: "We The People Are Greater Than Fear." Next to them were other women holding their own hand-made signs aloft: "Our Bodies, Our Minds, Our POWER" and "Make Racists Afraid Again."

Electoral politics, anti-nationalist and pro-immigrant rights politics, anti-racism, pro-reproductive rights, anti-misogyny, pro-democracy commitments—their intersections in contemporary feminism were made physically visible in the 2017 Women's Marches. Each, however, was marked by its own particular local resonances. Interestingly, however, militarism was not an explicit concern voiced by most of the Women's March participants around the world. It could have been that the withdrawal of most of their own countries' NATO-commanded troops from Iraq and Afghanistan had somewhat dulled protestors' awareness of militarism in its most immediately bloody forms. By January 2017, few flag-draped soldiers' coffins were being flown home to Canada, the United States, Denmark, Sweden, or Britain. On the other hand, many women who had been long active in such transnational feminist anti-war groups as WILPF and Women in Black saw the marches as reinforcing their own analyses and activism. Moreover, the plight of women and men who had become refugees as they fled current war zones—in Syria, Yemen, Somalia, Sudan, Congo—were on the minds of many January marchers. Rather than signs and speeches declaring opposition to war and militarism, many marchers in different countries seemed to challenge what feminists have pointed to as the gendered seeds of war and militarism: that is, masculinization; nationalism; racism; xenophobia; and misogyny.[24]

The British Women's March participants were the marchers whose current concerns were most widely compared to those preoccupying American marchers. In June 2016, seven months before the Women's March, Britain had held a national referendum posing a stark question: should Britain remain within the 28-nation European Union or leave it? The so-called "Brexit" campaign featured many of the same contentious social issues that exercised presidential-campaign American voters: immigration, globalization, jobs, and national sovereignty. Ultimately, a majority of British voters, 52 percent, cast their ballots for "Leave."

Some commentators viewed this victory for "Britain First" nationalists as a boost for Donald Trump's own electoral chances. Brexit seemed to make his nationalist and xenophobic rhetoric appear, if not more legitimate, then at least more "normal." After Brexit, it was harder to portray Donald Trump and his ideas as beyond the political pale.

Analyzing Britain's EU referendum balloting, the demographic voting differences that stood out were by age and region: a wide majority of younger voters chose "Remain," while a majority of older voters chose "Leave"; at the same time, majorities of voters in Scotland, Northern Ireland, and metropolitan London cast their ballots to "Remain," while most Britons living in Wales and in other parts of England opted for "Leave." The referendum's gender patterns were quite different. In contrast to recent parliamentary elections, when a higher proportion of British women than men voted Labour, Britain's 2016 Brexit vote seemed to have produced a negligible gender gap.[25]

This apparent lack of a gender voting gap did not mean, though, that the Brexit campaign had no gendered causes or consequences. For instance, Loughborough University researchers tracking whose voices were being heard and whose were not, in the weeks of heated debate leading up to the June vote, found that, of all the television appearances devoted to the EU issue, only 16 percent were by women. Eighty-four percent of television appearances that shaped the public's understanding of the issues at stake were by men.[26]

During the spring 2016 campaign, British feminists tried to raise a warning flag: leaving the EU would have negative consequences for many British women. At the time of Brexit there still existed a stubborn pay gap between British women and men: on average, over their entire working careers, British men earned 13.9 percent more than did British women. It was forty-six years since the enactment of Britain's historic Equal Pay Act. Nonetheless, owing to a lack of meaningful maternity leave and affordable childcare, together with persistent channeling of women into the lowest-paid caring professions and practices of outright sex discrimination in work, the gender pay gap actually was widening.[27] British feminist supporters of a "Remain" vote noted that the British policy-making establishment was still, on the eve of the Brexit vote, largely white and predominantly not just male but masculinist in its collective outlook. This made it unlikely that most members of the national political elite knew first-hand or genuinely cared about diverse women's lived realities. In parliament, only 29.6 percent of members of the House of Commons were women. A mere 3 percent were women of color. It was, these feminists argued, Brussels-issued EU directives that pushed reluctant British elites to strengthen and expand their country's gender equality actions.[28] Yet, with the loudest voices heard during the campaign focusing on immigration, these facts did not get much air time.

In the wake of the June 2016 "Leave" victory, and while Britain's way forward was still murky, the Fawcett Society called on the nation's policy-makers not to "turn back the clock on women's rights."[29] In fourteen towns and cities Britons took to the streets on January 21, 2017 to join the Sister Marches: Barnstable, Belfast, Bristol, Cardiff, Edinburgh, the Isle of Eigg, Lancaster, Leeds, Lerwick, Liverpool, London, Manchester, Shipley, and St. Austell. Many marchers were motivated by a sense that sexism, both institutional and everyday, was alive and well in contemporary Britain.[30] Many saw it as fueled by Brexit and the Trump presidency, which together represented an unrealistic and dangerous shrunken form of nationalist identity, a pulling-up of the proverbial drawbridge.

Despite historically widespread expressions of resistance to so many interlocking forms of gendered abuse, exclusion, and inequity, almost none of the marchers named patriarchy as the villain. Yet patriarchy served as both the glue for holding the separate parts of patriarchy together in a coherent whole, and as the fuel to propel it forward, even in times of extraordinary resistance.

Patriarchy. How passé. How "yesterday."

Patriarchy evokes either the hypocritically strait-laced Victorians or, more recently, the adulterous, martini-drinking "Mad Men." It doesn't seem to evoke the lives we live today. Rather, one thinks of patriarchy as a rather heavy-handed term that a generation ago Second Wave feminists painted on their protest signs.

Think again.

Patriarchy is as current as Brexit, Donald Trump, and nationalist political parties. It is as *au courant* as Twitter, hedge funds, and weaponized drones. Patriarchy is not old-fashioned; it is as hip as football millionaires and Silicon Valley start-ups.

The fact that patriarchy is a term so many people shy away from using is one of the things that enables it to survive.

Patriarchy is everyday sexism, but it is more than everyday sexism. Patriarchy embraces misogyny, but relies on more than misogyny. Patriarchy produces gender inequality, but its consequences run deeper than gender inequality.

Patriarchy is a system—a dynamic web—of particular ideas and relationships. That system of interwoven ideas and relationships is not brittle; it is not static. Patriarchy can be updated and modernized. It is stunningly adaptable. That is the sense in which it is useful, I think, to talk about patriarchy as "sustainable."

Today, we think of "sustainability" as a positive thing, as a reference point with which to measure whether any practice or policy is worthy of our support. Thus the newest United Nations goals for international development are called the Sustainable Development Goals ("SDGs" to UN insiders). To be positively sustainable, a project should meet more than short-term objectives; it should be designed for the long term. To be sustainable, an undertaking should eschew narrow self-interests, instead providing benefits for the widest possible constituency. To be sustainable, a policy should be earth-centric, not merely human-centric.

- Planting cash crops dependent on soil-degrading chemicals is not sustainable.
- Designing a transport system that continues to rely on fossil-fuel-guzzling automobiles and trucks is not sustainable.
- Crafting a national development plan that raises the Gross National Product while widening the gap between the rich minority and the poor majority is not sustainable.
- Negotiating a formula for ending a war that satisfies only the armed men at the table will not create a sustainable peace.

Sustainability, however, is only as positive as the thing we choose to perpetuate. "Sustainable patriarchy" sounds odd, but it is not a contradiction in terms. It simply describes how a system of ideas and relationships that so many women have risked their reputations and lives to challenge has, nonetheless, managed to survive.

Describing patriarchy's stubborn survival and its remarkable adaptability is not to drape it in a mantle of unassailability. The concept of "sustainable patriarchy" is not intended to deepen despair or feed resignation. Quite the opposite. Exposing the ways patriarchal systems are being perpetuated today will enable us to more effectively challenge and dismantle them. The ideas and relationships that comprise any patriarchal system are multiple, but knowable. They are not mysterious. They are not abstracted from daily life. Patriarchy is what we live.

Patriarchal ideas include both beliefs (that is, how we explain how the world works) and values (what we deem is worthy, good, attractive, as well as what we find unworthy, bad, distasteful). Both can be appealing—and in fact are appealing, not only to most men, but to a lot of women. That appeal is one of the things that sustains it. When we explore what persuaded so many American women to vote for Trump in the 2016 presidential election—or to support conservative parties in Britain, Poland, Chile, Japan, or Australia —we should think seriously about the appeals and rewards of patriarchy for diverse women.

Patriarchal beliefs include understandings about whether sex is fixed at birth, whether gender is synonymous with sex, whether women and men are "naturally" different, whether maleness is inherently rational, while femaleness is inherently emotional. Patriarchal beliefs also include understandings about whether humans of different races are "naturally" ranked in a hierarchy, whether the core elements of human societies are biological families, and whether the world is a dangerous place that necessitates men acting as the protectors of women. Patriarchal beliefs include, as well, potent notions of fate and inevitability. A shrug of one's shoulders can express a belief.

In other words, our beliefs are how we go about making sense of our complex surroundings and the wider universe in which we live. For instance, current arguments about transgender people and about climate change have starkly exposed deeply held conflicting beliefs. Likewise, learning only now, fifty years after their achievements, that African American women mathematicians were crucial players in the creation of the US space program can be unnerving to many people.[31] Perhaps our surprise when we learn this history reveals that, until now, we had believed that Black women did not have the capabilities to master advanced mathematics.

Patriarchal values are supported by patriarchal beliefs, but are intended more explicitly to steer behavior. Thus we tend to make *values* the topics of our debates among friends, families, and political parties, even if it is our differing *beliefs* that ignite the deepest conflicts with each other. Among the patriarchal values that have been most contentious are those assigning more worth to reason than to emotion, those which bestow inherent worth on traditions, and those which prioritize family loyalty over all other sorts of commitment.

To rank governments on the basis of whether they are militarily sophisticated and paternalistically authoritarian towards their citizens also demonstrates our absorption of patriarchal values. Patriarchal values often include admiration for what are imagined to be manly forms of leadership, and, as a patriarchal complement, admiration chiefly for women who devote themselves first and foremost to mothering. Thus, to anyone embracing such patriarchal values, hearing Liberian Leymah Gbowee praised for her successful mobilization of the Liberian women's peace movement, without any reference to her behavior as a wife or a mother, can feel uncomfortable. Authoritarian values are commonly thought to characterize leaders who themselves aspire to be authoritarian in their own wielding of power. Across many cultures, leaders' authoritarian inclinations are intertwined with their presumed manliness. Contempt for femininity—even while showing off one's "winning way with women"—is often coupled with masculinized authoritarian leadership. This insight is notable in feminist explorations of authoritarianism.

No continent or culture has a monopoly on authoritarian leaders. Zimbabwe's president, Robert Mugabe, has often been described as a proto-typical authoritarian ruler. Egypt's former general and current president, Abdel Fattah el-Sisi, and China's president, Xi Jinping, may sit on top of quite dissimilar state systems, but both exhibit distinctly authoritarian modes of leadership. So too does Russian president Vladimir Putin and his Middle East ally, Syrian President Bashar al-Assad.[32] In 2017, Turkey's president, Recep Tayyip Erdoğan, held a national referendum which narrowly passed a constitutional amendment that in effect enabled him to wield state power in a more authoritarian manner.

Of course, women who become leaders can absorb and advocate for authoritarian values, though the gendered credentials are distinctive. One thinks of Margaret Thatcher and Indira Gandhi. Both women were admired for their allegedly masculinized skills. "The only man in the room," according to each of their male admirers.

Many American Women's March participants voiced alarm at Donald Trump's apparent efforts to transform the US presidency into an authoritarian post. They saw evidence of his valuing a sort of leadership that was dismissive of the presidency's relationships with co-equal legislative and court branches. He appeared to value a sort of masculinized authority that would not be constrained by the deliberately complex system of American constitutionalism. To accept such structural constraints, in his mind, it seemed, bordered on becoming feminized.

It is a mistake, however, to think of authoritarian values as adhering just to a certain kind of leader. Authoritarian values are embraced by those men and women far from the centers of power who, nonetheless, admire the type of manly leader who presents himself as "strong." That is, among its followers, authoritarianism can take the form of submissiveness. The iconic version of masculinized submission to an authoritarian leader is the "loyal lieutenant." But there are other masculinized versions as well: the fawning courtier, the self-interested crony, the aspiring wannabe, the proverbial "foot soldier." To be an authoritarian voter is to be someone—of any gender—who yearns for a manly man (or a suitably masculinized woman) to take firm hold on the reins of power and sweep away all the frustrating complexities of constitutional checks and balances. Such a voter hopes that this leader will eschew the time-consuming give-and-take of democratic debate and compromise. To absorb authoritarian values in one's role as citizen fosters admiration for a leader who dismisses the constraints of law and the messiness that is the characteristic of a genuinely open public arena. Vladimir Putin, Recep Tayyip Erdoğan and Donald Trump have each had their fervent admirers, even when those admirers do not garner direct benefits from that leader's rule. Though they might imagine themselves to be defiantly individualistic, these admirers are authoritarian in both the values they espouse and the relationships in which they take comfort.

Values and beliefs often capture our attention more readily than *patriarchal relationships*. Patriarchal relationships have to be minutely observed over time. That calls for stamina, patience, and attentiveness. Patriarchal relationships are hard to reveal in a snapshot and only occasionally appear on a formal organizational chart—X reports to Y, while Z has the power to promote or fire Y. Most lived relationships are nuanced. They are made visible not just through speeches, memos, minutes, punches, gunshots, or exchanges of cash—though tracking each of these can be revealing. Relationships are charted by taking careful note of small gestures, unrecorded silences, and little-noticed absences. The artful rendition of relationships has drawn thousands of readers to the novels of Jane Austen and Elena Ferrante. That is why we binge-watch *House of Cards* and *The Crown.*

To say that patriarchy has proved remarkably adaptable is not to argue that there have been no significant successes in challenging it. Patriarchy would not *need* to constantly adapt if those anti-patriarchal successes had not been achieved. The forcing of men by women to accept their casting ballots on equal terms with men, in countries as different as Sweden, South Africa, and Brazil, has compelled patriarchal men and women to find new ways to ensure the privileging of masculinity in governance. Similarly, women in countries as disparate as Samoa, Turkey, and Britain who have managed to drag the practice of wife-beating out of the domestic shadows, and compel reluctant governments to treat it as a crime, have motivated patriarchy's adherents to craft new strategies for intimidating women.

It has been this combination of feminist achievement and patriarchy's adaptability that has required women's movements across the world to keep reinventing themselves. To grapple with an adaptable patriarchy takes time, energy, and ever more diverse alliances. Patriarchy's beneficiaries count on us getting tired.

Patriarchal systems—those dynamic webs of beliefs, values, and relationships—have to be able to adapt in ways that make them look new, reformed, "up-to-date," occasionally even revolutionary. Their advocates have to perform these repeated facelifts while sustaining patriarchy's essential core: the privileging of particular forms of masculinity over despised masculinities and over all forms of femininity. A few select women can be let into the boardroom—or onto the television sportscast or into the law school—but on (usually unwritten and denied) conditions: that those few women do not insist that many more women of diverse races join them; that those allowed inside internalize masculinized ways of thinking (about profits, war, sexuality, inequality); or, by contrast, that those few selected women act out a form of patriarchal femininity that complements but does not supplant masculinized privilege.

There is an alternative process for perpetuating patriarchal beliefs, values, and relationships, which is to turn what used to be a site of masculinized privilege into a site of feminized marginalization. The classic example is bank clerking. In Dickens's time, to be a bank clerk was to be a respectable manly man with a foot on the lower rung of the patriarchal ladder; by the early twenty-first century, bank clerking has become feminized and the ladder leads nowhere.[33] Similarly, the anchoring of television news programs used to be an exclusively male job. It, too, has been feminized in many countries in ways that have sucked much of the authority out of the position. Likewise, military male commanders deciding that certain once-masculinized roles could be feminized, without risking the reputation of the military as a site for men to prove their manliness, is as old as uniformed female soldiers serving as secretaries for male officers. Recently, for example, the US military has taken steps to replace male soldiers with female soldiers at war zone checkpoints.

Women are under-represented in all but two of the world's national legislatures, those of Bolivia and Rwanda.[34] They are making gains, however, at the same time as many governments, in the name of "anti-terrorism," are investing more power in their security officials. It may not be fantastical, then, to wonder if one day elected legislators will become so powerless that patriarchs will encourage the feminization of legislatures, while real power will be wielded by men (and a few select women) occupying masculinized posts atop the treasury, the military, and the security and intelligence agencies.

Updating patriarchy requires more than perpetuating domination, intimidation, and submission. It also requires reproducing certain relationships that on the surface look benign: gratitude, attachment, dependence, competition, suspicion, trust, loyalty, and even compassion. That can make it easy to slip into patriarchal complicity without intending to or even realizing the implications of one's feelings and actions. Marching in creative, energizing, inclusive protests matters. The experience can remind participants who are trying to resist patriarchy in all its guises that they are not alone. If such public demonstrations against patriarchy stem from authentically grassroots initiatives, they can also simultaneously remind participants of the full array of issues, fears, identities, and aspirations that have to be acknowledged in order to effectively stymie the updating of patriarchy. Everyone has to join in everyone else's chants.

At the same time, however, feminist investigations of contemporary patriarchy reveal that it will take more than public demonstrations to stop patriarchy in its tracks. It will take humble, clear-eyed reflections on one's own possible complicities in its perpetuation.

CHAPTER TWO

Syrian Women Resist
Peace Table Patriarchy

As Russian and Syrian government planes bombed Aleppo into rubble during the early weeks of 2017, residents by the thousand fled their city, historically one of the Middle East's most celebrated centers of art and commerce. With most civilian women being forced to flee while all-male Opposition militias retreated, and with the arrival of the all-male troops of the Assad government and its Iranian and Hezbollah allies, Aleppo was becoming hour by hour not only more militarized, but also more masculinized.

It may seem inconceivable that during years of brutal violence any women could carve out any space for civil activism. In the aftermath of the government's suppression of the non-violent pro-democracy movement of 2011, neighboring powers calculated their own interests, local men joined disparate armed Opposition groups, and thousands of foreign male fighters arrived in Syria as recruits for both pro-Assad and rebel ultra-conservative militias. At the same time, though scarcely reported, many Syrian civilian women committed themselves to staying as long as they could inside Syria to do the mostly invisible work of holding their battered wartime communities together. The war dragged on, however, and more and more Syrian women were compelled to flee—to neighboring Turkey, Jordan, Lebanon, and Iraq, as well as Europe; a trickle made it to the United States. By the end of 2015, with the war in its fourth year, the UN High Commission for Refugees reported that 4.9 million Syrians had been turned into refugees, as they fled across national borders. An additional 6.6 million Syrians had been forced from their homes by the war but had remained within Syria's borders, thereby becoming "internally displaced persons."

Some Syrian women became refugee activists. They campaigned, for instance, for girls to stay in school. Due to wartime insecurity and dislocation, girls' education was becoming ever more tightly bound to debates over child marriage. UNICEF tracked the alarming rise in child marriages among Syrian refugees: the rate tripled between 2011 and 2015. Mothers and fathers (not always in agreement, but with fathers having the final say) were choosing to marry off their young daughters in the hope that they might ensure their daughters' security (referred to locally as *sutra*) or lessen the family's already heavy financial burden, or both. In this way, despite many parents' well-meaning intent, wartime displacement was serving to sustain patriarchy.

It is worth pausing here to take a second look at language. Independently from the practice of patriarchy, the very choice of language can perpetuate patriarchal beliefs. Commonly used by officials of international agencies and governments, as well as by staffers of non-governmental human rights and humanitarian aid organizations, many of whom are dedicated to improving girls' and women's lives, this familiar phrase, "child marriages," may be helping to sustain patriarchy.

How does this work?

"Child marriages" implies that boys as well as girls are offered up in marriage by their parents while they are still minors. This is true. However, by adopting the phrase "child marriages" one is suggesting that boys are just as likely as girls to be married while still in their childhood, and this is not true. For instance, researchers for UNICEF concluded, in their detailed 2016 report *A Study on Early Marriage in Jordan, 2014,* that, among both Jordanian children and Syrian refugee children living in Jordan, less than even one half of one percent of the children married were boys. That is, in reality, these are not "child marriages." They are *girl* marriages. Each of us helps to sustain patriarchal ideas and practices when we hide the workings of gendered inequities behind a curtain of ungendered language. And, when we hide patriarchy, we are sustaining it.

As the violence continued, Syrian refugee girls as young as fifteen were being married to men ten years, even twenty years their senior. Girls dropping out of school were *both* the cause *and* the consequence of this particular gendering of child marriage: if school was deemed by parents unimportant for girls, or attendance too dangerous, girls were then imagined by male suitors to be available for marriage. At the same time, if parents considered marriage the best option for a young daughter who was still attending school, then she would be taken out of school in order to be married. Pregnancy and motherhood usually followed quite soon after marriage, so that chances for married girls to re-enter school quickly faded.

Women and girls have become civil society activists within Syrian refugee communities. For example, Muzoon Almellehan, an eighteen-year-old Syrian, who fled the war with her parents in 2011, became an outspoken campaigner for refugee girls' right to go to school and stay in school. The site for her activism was Jordan's sprawling Zaatari refugee camp. Lives in Zaatari, as they are in every refugee settlement, are gendered: women and men do not experience becoming a refugee identically; nor do girls and boys. Marriage, poverty, work, sexuality, physical insecurity, health, domestic decision-making, education, and access to food —each was gendered before a Syrian family experienced wartime displacement; each has been gendered—often in unexpected ways—in the midst of it. That is, when one becomes a refugee, one does not suddenly, miraculously become "ungendered." It has taken years of research and pressuring for transnational feminist advocates to get humanitarian aid and refugee agencies to even partially absorb this reality, let alone to act on it.

Muzoon Almellehan found that if she tied her campaigning efforts to those of the better-known young Nobel Peace Prize laureate and Pakistani girl activist Malala Yousafzai, more people would pay attention. But Almellehan was wary. She had learned from experience that media and government attention rarely translated into sustained meaningful support for women and girls. Celebrating girl activists, putting them on magazine and book covers, bestowing prizes on them and inviting them to appear on TV interview shows can be a way to avoid actually meeting their demands. As for political attention, in December 2016 *Ms.* magazine quoted an alert Almellehan: "Sometimes I think leaders make promises when the world is watching.... I want them to know that Malala and I will keep watching. We have to make sure that, when politicians and diplomats make promises, they do not forget them when they leave." As Muzoon warns, empty celebrity, even of girls' and women's advocates, can sustain patriarchy.

This acute wariness by women civil society activists was on collective display when the United Nations hosted Syrian peace negotiations in Geneva, Switzerland in year three of the devastating war. I was fortunate to be invited by the Women's International League for Peace and Freedom (WILPF) to come to Geneva in January 2014 to serve as an observer of this peace negotiation effort. WILPF activists were wary. They had seen too many peace negotiations become yet a new round in masculinized politics. Today, I look back and see that being there taught me new lessons about what it has taken to sustain patriarchy.

Perhaps the lessons to be learned will be thrown into sharper relief if I recall this Geneva experience in the form of a diary, for, as so often happens, feminist learning doesn't come in a dramatic flash; it accumulates over hours and days of listening and observing and reflecting.

DAY I: PRELUDE TO THE SYRIAN
PEACE TALKS IN GENEVA

Geneva is a beautiful city straddling the far end of the very large Lake Geneva. On one side of the bridge is the old city, with shops, cafés, museums. On the opposite side of the lake, where I was staying, are modern apartments, the big train station, halal butcher's shops, and acres of glass high-rise international agency offices: the UN High Commission for Refugees, the UN International Labour Organization, the UN Human Rights Council, as well as the offices of Doctors Without Borders, the International Committee of the Red Cross, and dozens more.

WILPF, my host, itself was the major transnational feminist organization with its headquarters in Geneva. Founded in 1915, in protest against the waging of World War I, WILPF was headed now by Madeleine Rees, a British feminist lawyer and one of the really smart feminist strategists who was pushing for women's rights to be taken seriously in UN peacekeeping operations and in the crucial post-conflict transitional political arrangements. WILPF was joined by MADRE, Code Pink, the International Civil Society Action Network (ICAN), and the Swedish feminist group Kvinna till Kvinna. Predicting (rightly) that the overwhelming majority of the UN, US, British and Russian officials, the chief coordinators of the official talks, would be men, and that their beliefs, values, and relationships would be masculinized, this alliance of transnational feminists created what they called "alternative peace negotiations," to model what non-patriarchal peace negotiations would look like. They made Syrian civil society women activists their principal invitees. Rees also invited two feminist Nobel laureates—from Northern Ireland (Mairead Maguire), and Iran (Shirin Ebadi). Over a cafeteria lunch, Ebadi explained that she had been forced to leave Iran once the government had forcibly closed down her law firm because of its work defending human rights advocates. With other Nobel women peace laureates, Shirin Ebadi and Mairead Maguire had created a Nobel Women's Initiative working internationally for peace.

Participants in these alternative peace negotiations gathered at the Graduate Institute, just a short walk from the UN offices. We sat in a big circle and dived into our first puzzle. How could women civil society activists persuade UN officials and the US and Russian co-conveners—as well as all the Syrian men invited to sit at the official peace talks table—to see that including only men who wielded guns (and the men with briefcases who had large armies behind them), plus a few token women, could not be a formula for a creating a sustainable peace? That is, how could feminists with years of experience in war zones convince masculinized officials that believing that "only men with guns can make peace" was false, and basing actions on that false belief was fruitless?

Over the last fifteen years, the government and international agency officials have learned how to say the polite, diplomatic things about caring about women in war zones—in public. But in practice they have gone on taking seriously only men with guns. Instead, the women who had come together here, as diverse as we/ they certainly were, agreed: the only productive formula for moving towards a sustainable peace (the word "sustainable" was used repeatedly—these were not "quick fix" sorts of thinkers) was to have seated at the official table (not as mere "observers") representatives of those women civil society activists inside Syria who knew what it would take to reweave the fabric of society. The term "civil society" was used by all the women gathered in Geneva to mean: NOT militias, NOT political parties, NOT groups representing any regime; to create a civil society is to create a society of genuine citizens, not subjects.

One Syrian woman active with civil society groups working inside Syria told us a story. Rim Turkmani was an astrophysics professor and local community organizer. She came from Homs, the Syrian city where the non-violent movement began in early 2011, calling on the Assad regime to open up politics for a more transparent, democratic process. She said that no one she had known in Homs had ever called village X "Shiite" or suburb Y "Sunni." She said: "I had a roommate and I didn't even know whether she was Shiite or Sunni. Who cared?" Turkmani blamed the divisive new trend in part on outsiders, for instance the Saudi, Turkish, Qatari, and Iranian governments, each of which was pouring money into Syria for their respective proxy fighters and political organizations for the sake of their own (competing) regional ambitions. When US and British officials also started seeing any Syrian with a peace proposal as "representing" a particular sect or party, they played into this destructive dynamic. It also, Turkmani told us, reinforced Assad's claim that only his regime represented "all Syrians," even though he had been playing the ethnicity and sectarian cards for years.

Listening to Rim's story, I was reminded of Iraqi feminists during the years of the US occupation (2003–10) saying that, the more the US officials insisted on seeing Iraq's troubles in sectarian and ethnic terms, the more Iraqis themselves, many of whom had friendships and neighborly and marital relations without ever employing such narrow identity boxes, began to think of themselves and their fellow citizens in these divisive terms.

DAY 2: OFFICIAL TALKS BEGIN

There was a brief glimpse of blue sky over Geneva in the morning. The snow-topped black mountains could be viewed across the lake. As I walked along the lakeside in the freezing wintry air, heading for the morning's meeting, I spied a couple of hardy Swiss people swimming.

The official UN-US-British-Russian-sponsored Syrian Peace Talks were due to start in the mountain resort of Montreux, outside Geneva. A busload of women set out there to unfurl banners calling for Syrian civil society women activists to be invited to take seats at the official negotiating table. There were to be three women in the Syrian Opposition's delegation and two on the Assad government's delegation. None of them, however, had been given a speaking role.

At the WILPF offices the previous evening, as soon as the names of the three women members of the Opposition delegation had been released, everyone around the crowded table had compared notes on what they knew of these women, who had been appointed by the male leaders of the Opposition Council. None of the three was known to be a civil society activist inside Syria. This posed one of the classic dilemmas experienced by women living in a patriarchal world: should feminists welcome the fact that at the last minute the men leading each of the warring sides had added a few women to their official rosters, or not? Was it authentic representation, or mere "window-dressing"? The Syrian women civil society activists and their transnational feminist supporters had never called for just *any* women to be included in the peace negotiations. They wanted Syrian women at the table who were actively involved "on the ground" inside Syria—women providing wartime aid, building community reconciliation—in order to contribute knowledge of what the majority of Syrian women wished for, for their own and their country's futures.

When pushing for genuine change inside a patriarchy, one must ask: can even a token be turned into something substantive?

Among all the women who had travelled to Geneva for the alternative peace negotiations were women from Syria, Italy, Bosnia, Sri Lanka, Northern Ireland, Britain, the United States, Turkey, Iran, Norway, Sweden, Western Sahara, France, Germany, Guatemala. Altogether, there were about eighty of us crowded good-naturedly into a room at the Geneva Graduate Institute. From what anyone could tell, only a few embassies had sent any staff to listen to these lively, informed discussions. A smattering of people from UN agencies came. No mainstream media journalists bothered to attend. Thus the story of the Syrian war and peace negotiations continued to be told by the mainstream media as if only men with guns and men from powerful governments mattered.

As official talks convened up the mountain, those of us gathering down below that same morning sat in layered circles of folding chairs. Women from multiple war zones past and current began to share lessons and caveats with Syrian women activists. Two Northern Irish women—Anne Patterson and Nobel Peace Prize laureate Mairead Maguire—said that the key to their success in getting women with genuinely representative (non-partisan) credentials into the meetings that eventually hammered out the 1998 Good Friday Agreement was years of organizing across the Catholic/Protestant and class divides. Women, they warned, had to muster the courage and stamina to join with women with whom they deeply disagreed, women whose sons had shot their own children. Out of this trust-building they created a non-party coalition to run for the posts as peace delegation representatives, and then to win enough popular votes to be eligible to "sit at the table." Anne and Mairead acknowledged that it could be discouraging for Syrian women to hear that it had taken them years. So they added: "Don't be daunted; find your own pace to fit your own Syrian conditions now."

Once inside the Northern Irish peace negotiations, Anne and Mairead recalled, the women's representatives refused to let the "men's egos" subvert the talks: when opposing male delegates threatened to walk out unless they got their own way, women from the women's coalition had talked them back to the table. Importantly, they insisted that into the substance of the formal peace agreement there had to be inserted commitments by all sides to create new public commissions, one on poverty, the other on women's rights. Once created, each commission was to be headed by a woman. That is, a peace agreement needed also to become a civil-society-rebuilding blueprint. Laying down weapons was not sufficient for reweaving a tattered social fabric.

Guatemalan feminist peace activist Luz Méndez spoke next. She told us that, initially, she had been on an official delegation of the anti-regime insurgents to the UN-brokered 1990s Guatemalan peace talks. Luz had been the sole woman at the table, along with twenty-eight men. But she had been simultaneously part of a network of local women's civil society groups and kept constantly in touch with them. That open channel of genuine communication had built trust between the official delegates at the talks and the wider Guatemalan citizenry, whose priority had been ending the violence. The formal channel had also allowed for creative ideas, especially from women civil society activists, to make their way into the official deliberations. Despite the positive elements of the final formal peace agreement, Luz warned us, post-war violence continued to tear Guatemalan society apart. Central to it was systematic violence against Guatemalan women: violence fueled not only by persistent poverty, but by the growing drug trade.

Sitting next to Luz was a Sri Lankan woman who had been active in organizing Sinhalese and Tamil women during, and since, the deadly twenty-five-year-long conflict in her country. She supported the advice of her Northern Irish and Guatemalan colleagues: when your first try at building trust among women of warring communities fails, don't give up.

DAY 2 CONTINUED: SYRIAN WOMEN SPEAK

First on the agenda after lunch was listening to two women from Bosnia; they reported that Bosnian women from Bosnia—and also those from Serbia and Croatia—had had scarcely any voice at all in the 1995 US-brokered Dayton Accords that had ended the devastating four-year war in the former Yugoslavia. Like the current Syrian talks, the masculinized Yugoslav negotiations had been held far from the society in conflict: at the Wright US Air Force base in Dayton, Ohio. As an aside, one of the Bosnian women commented that it was noteworthy that these *peace* talks were held on a military base. Looking back over a decade of post-war experience, the Bosnian women concluded that the most damaging element of the Dayton Accords was that they had included a new constitution. It was bad enough that the peace negotiations had excluded local women activists (and scores of women's groups did exist in early-1990s Yugoslavia, one of the most prominent being the Belgrade Women in Black), and that these constitutional arrangements had not been put to an open popular vote; but even worse was that, with the US government taking the lead, the insertion of a new constitution into the peace agreement had meant that ethnic differences among the women and men of the now-fragmented Yugoslavia were hardened into legal and institutional structures. This had made Bosnian activist women's fifteen-year-long effort to build a genuine post-war civil society, one that superseded alleged ethnic identities, almost impossible.

Three women from the Western Sahara shared their own experiences with us. They stressed how *in*effective all the peace talks had been between the Moroccan government and the people of the Western Sahara. Women had been totally excluded. Consequently, over the years—they were now in Year 14 of making their lives in what had been intended to be temporary refugee camps—women active in local affairs had concentrated on organizing women inside the camps and on getting women into positions of some influence within the camps' leadership structures. The women told us: "No one thinks about us any more; the Western Saharan conflict is not on anyone's mind."

During a short coffee break I chatted with a woman from one of the big Geneva-based international aid organizations, who had come to listen. Her specific job in the organization was to ensure that her colleagues' work was "gender-sensitive." (I cannot give the organization's name because, given how few staff in that building were assigned the job of monitoring gender equity, it would be too easy to trace her.) This woman was fuming. Only the day before, she had received an email from one of her senior male supervisors telling her that she should take care of the procurement of sanitary pads for delivery to women refugees. But this committed staff woman had nothing to do with procurement—that was the job of an entirely different department. As explanation for his odd, inappropriate request, this senior man had simply told her: "I don't do women."

Fueled by coffee, we began to listen carefully to four Syrian activist women now living in exile. Two women described an effort they'd launched here in Geneva to bring Syrians of all backgrounds and political affiliations together over Syrian food, using recipes from all regions of the country. No talk of politics, religion, or even of the conflict was allowed. The point was just to be together, to remind each other how much they shared as Syrians.

These Syrian women—as women from any country would—had quite dissimilar understandings of what their society had been like before the outbreak of violence in 2011—that is, before the Assad regime chose military force as its response to the non-violent pro-democracy public demonstrations calling on the government to reform. Some Syrian women now living outside Syria, for instance, recalled a pre-war society in which they had felt secure: "Women could walk at night in Damascus without any fear." Other Syrian exiled women, by contrast, recalled that, while before 2011 there wasn't overt violence, there was systematic political repression aimed at anyone who dared to be critical of the government. Even among this handful of women, there existed quite different understandings of history and of "security."

One young Syrian woman, now in exile in France, gave an example of how the less visible violence had been transformed by 2012 into a more overt kind. "I had never been political. I was leading a pretty comfortable life. Then, one day, after soldiers had started shooting civilians, I saw Assad on television laughing as the news of the killings was reported. That was it for me. I decided I had to do something." She joined a small group of women who were trying to provide the simplest forms of support to those families who had lost members to the violence. At Easter, she and a friend had decided to distribute chocolate Easter eggs to children in these grieving families. "We wrote messages both from the Koran and from the Gospels on the eggs." But while on their rounds they were arrested by police, and taken to a prison. "They put us in a cell next to a torture room, where we could hear other prisoners pleading to be killed rather than be subjected to more torture." Eventually she was released, and she had fled to Paris, where she launched an online radio station for Syrians.

Suddenly, there was a commotion outside the glass wall of the room. Cheerful welcomes and much hugging. Syrian women from *inside* Syria had just managed to arrive! This was no small feat—receiving international funding for the trip, getting through checkpoints, obtaining visas, crossing state borders...

The four newly arrived Syrian women took chairs in the inner circle, where they were joined by Madeleine Rees of WILPF and Swedish activist Lena Ag of Kvinna till Kvinna. I was asked to serve as moderator. Our task was to outline the particular obstacles to women civil society activists getting a place at the peace talks table. Madeleine, with direct experience in Bosnia, where she had served as Mary Robinson's Special Representative for the UN Office of the High Commissioner for Human Rights (OHCHR), urged each of us to subvert the conventional militarizing, masculinizing narrative everywhere we heard it. She pushed us to go further, to articulate an alternative and more realistic peace-building narrative: civil society activists, many of them women, bring to the table their knowledge of local conditions and their commitment to creating sustainable peace and meaningful security in ways that produce more genuine security. This has the best chance of producing an agreement that fosters authentic citizenship and political transparency.

Lena's contribution underscored these points. She described Kvinna till Kvinna's cross-national, detailed study of the dynamics that today continue to favor masculinized peace negotiations. She reminded us that these dynamics persist in spite of the vote in the year 2000 by the UN Security Council's members (including, of course, the United States and Russia) to adopt UN Security Council Resolution 1325 on women, peace and security (which many women in the room referred to simply as "1325").

Resolution 1325 was ground-breaking. It committed both the agencies of the UN and every UN member state to take explicit actions to ensure that women were not just treated as "victims," but counted as serious players. Resolution 1325, that is, has committed the UN and all UN member states to ensure that women have an effective voice in all peace agreement processes, in all post-agreement transitional political arrangements, and in all ongoing post-war state reforms and peace-building development. And yet, the key political players at these Syrian negotiations, and in so many recent peace processes, had marginalized women civil society representatives. Lena reminded us that this was in flagrant violation of the UN's own formal commitments.

The Syrian women who had just recently arrived then gave nuanced accounts of what women had been experiencing, but also of what women activists were doing in the midst of the ever-escalating violence. With the support of Karama, a Cairo-based women's rights group, some of them had formed the Syrian Women's Forum for Peace. Mouna Ghanem, a public health professional, had been among the Forum's co-founders. They had tried to bring together the scattered women's groups working locally inside Syria. Ghanem said that many Syrian women activists were beginning to be familiar with 1325, and were starting to see this UN resolution as bestowing international legitimacy on their own demands for inclusion in the peace talks.

Beyond demanding negotiation participation for women, these Syrian civil society activists—many of them trained in law, social work, and medicine—had been busy delivering humanitarian aid, neighborhood by neighborhood; they had been documenting violations of human rights; and they had created micro-ceasefires that could allow food and medical supplies intermittently to reach Syrians isolated by violence. To carry out effective local actions, they explained, one had to be attentive to changing local conditions. For instance, in one city neighborhood there might be five thousand armed fighters, most of them locally recruited, surrounded by twenty thousand civilians. In that instance, local people—many of whom knew the male fighters amongst them personally—could wield significant influence, pressing for a local ceasefire. By contrast, if the violence had escalated to a point where living in a neighborhood had become intolerable, forcing thousands of ordinary residents to flee, then the fighters might number five thousand, but the local residents might have been reduced to, say, two thousand. Under those conditions, negotiating even a short-lived ceasefire became unlikely.

Each of the four Syrian women activists said that they had concluded that women in Syria, no matter how difficult their immediate situations, "could not be passive." They insisted that, despite the spiraling sexual assaults on and kidnapping of women perpetrated by those warring men who saw women as mere currency in their rivalries with other men, Syrian women should not be imagined by the international media and agencies, nor by us, nor by themselves, as mere victims. Syrian women, in all their diversity, were people with a stake in the direction their country took; they were people with skills and knowledge. Syrian women were *citizens*.

That night, Code Pink participants screened documentary films by feminist filmmakers, including Abigail Disney's much-acclaimed documentary, *Pray the Devil Back to Hell*. The film documents how Liberian women managed, against all odds, to build a grassroots women's movement in the midst of violence. Its activists decided not to wait to be invited into the Liberian peace talks. Instead, led by Leymah Gbowee, they dramatically forced their way into the masculinized negotiations and successfully pressed warring tribal male factions to reach a sustainable cease-fire. Several people at the Geneva gathering wondered out loud if similar direct popular action by Syrian women was going to be the only strategy that would compel the Syrian male-led warring sides to prioritize peace instead of their own political survivals.

DAYS 3 AND 4

The morning's *International New York Times* was full of the news of the rocky, acrimonious start of the official Syrian peace talks up in the mountain resort of Montreux. Not a single woman was mentioned or quoted. This, despite dozens of peace activist women who had stood outside the talks holding signs calling for women's meaningful inclusion in the negotiations.

Down the mountain in Geneva the Syrian women activists held meetings with officials of the UN and several governments. The Norwegians were especially supportive, as were some British officials. None of this, however, got any Syrian civil society activists a seat at the negotiating table.

In all the discussions, these Syrian women activists under-scored the importance of creating civil society *during* wartime. They reminded us at every turn that, while Syrian women had organized in the 1930s–60s, in the last forty years there had not been space for civil society in Syria. The Assad (Senior and Junior) regimes had systematically sucked all the air out of civic space. For almost two generations, to be "political" in Syria had been shrunk to mean solely to be part of, or complicit with, the regime. To be anything other than supportive, complicit, or passive had been, in the Assad regimes' view, to be a "terrorist."

These challenges notwithstanding, Syrian women activists had created the beginnings of a civil society—citizens' action independent of the regime, independent of any armed group, independent of any party machine or sectarian hierarchy. They had done this by acting locally, by fulfilling civic needs that the government would not address, and that the male-led armed groups either could not or would not take seriously. Delivering food and medical supplies to displaced people within Syria— people (a majority of whom today are women with their dependent children, which is quite different from the patriarchal elision of "women and children") who had been forced to flee their homes because of violence—had become the principal space in which Syrian women could act as genuine citizens. It had not *only* been women who had been doing this work, the Syrian activists told us, but men had either been conscripted by the government's military, or become fighters for the Opposition, or gone into hiding, or been wounded or killed. Thus it had been women who, in the midst of escalating violence, had taken the lead in most Syrian civil society groups.

UN and government officials resistant to women activists' demands for seats at the negotiation table lectured the Syrian women who met with them, offering this collective advice: "It's too early. You're not ready. You aren't organized. You don't have a plan."

In response, the Syrian activist women who had made it to Geneva countered: "We have built networks of women active locally. We are ready. In fact we are more prepared for peace than most of the men at the table. And we do have a plan."

The plan comprised of a series of steps in order of priority. The first was a ceasefire. The second was the withdrawal of all foreign fighters and the immediate cessation of all import of weapons. Both of these steps were intended to make the third step possible: the delivery of humanitarian aid to the country's most desperate cities and towns. Beyond the delivery of aid, they called for women to be represented in all post-conflict institution-building plans, and for the prosecution of all acts of violence against women.

Several changes marked the year-by-year unfolding of the Syrian conflict. The Syrian women activists told us that each of these wartime changes had been *gendered*. Women had been prominent in the leadership of the initial non-violent pro-democracy demonstrations in early 2011. As the violence escalated, women's activist visibility had receded: as militarization spread, so did the masculinization of Syrian political life. Many of these women had been early pro-democracy leaders who had to flee abroad; those activists who stayed inside Syria had turned to less visible local humanitarian work, which too often is erroneously imagined to be outside of political life. As the formal UN peace talks began in early 2014, as tenuous as they clearly were, Syrian activist women once again were becoming more visibly political.

There was a second change that occurred in the middle of war: transformations of Syrian families and the Syrian economy—the two changes, of course, are always connected. The growth of the fighting forces and the resultant spread of violence had produced more and more women-led households. This change should not be read as a rollback of patriarchy. Just as women had become more relied upon to provide for the economic survival of families, so their own economic opportunities had shrunk. Meanwhile many male fighters were being paid for fighting—not much, but enough so that they began to see fighting as an economic activity. In addition, some Syrian local village leaders had begun turning armed checkpoints into money-spinners; setting these up around their villages allowed these local leaders to collect fees from any passing vehicle. In this way, some people had begun to have a personal economic stake in the continuation of the armed conflict.

Thirdly, as the conflict became more violent, and as the number of masculinized armed groups—Syrian and foreign, pro-Assad and anti-Assad, Iranian, Turkish, American, and Russian—proliferated, men's targeting of women had become more pronounced. Trafficking of women and girls, sexual assaults on women, forced early marriages of girls, arrests and torture of women, tightening of control of women's behavior for the sake of ideological goals—all had increased between mid-2011 and early 2014.

That is, "war" is not a static gendered condition. Armed conflicts morph; the forms of and expressions of and responses to patriarchy change. A peace negotiation that ignores these changes—that is hammered out by people who are deeply uncurious about these changes—will produce a peace agreement that will not sustain peace but perpetuate patriarchy.

DAY 5: LAST BUT NOT FINAL

The transnational feminist groups that were in regular contact with Syrian civil society activists provided them with official contacts, with media outlets for their analyses and plans, with funds for travel so they could meet with each other, and with chances to trade knowledge and strategies with women who had experienced other wars and pushed open other masculinized closed doors. The women active in a range of transnational feminist groups—WILPF, Code Pink, Women in Black, Women Living Under Muslim Law, Kvinna till Kvinna, MADRE, Equality Now, Karama, ICAN, as well as US-based women's peace groups such as WAND—all have been constantly learning and reflecting. They have had to learn how to be supportive without being presumptuous, how to facilitate without becoming the "story" themselves. It was instructive to witness this ongoing alliance-making among reflective feminists in the most daunting of political environments.

Friday's front page of the *International New York Times* (January 24, 2014) featured a photo of a Syrian woman standing in the middle of a rubble-strewn street in Aleppo. She had spontaneously put her hand up to cover her mouth as bombs had fallen. As I looked at her, I thought: *Who is representing you here at the Geneva Peace Talks?*

As so often happens in the mainstream media, and in even some allegedly alternative media, a woman is made the subject of a news photo, with a brief caption underneath, but then she vanishes. The story goes on with no further reference to her experiences and ideas. That is patriarchal journalism. The *Times* story featuring this appalled Syrian woman turned away from her and focused on the "scramble" to keep the faltering peace talks alive; it was a story about men, rival men, mediating official men, but all men—the UN envoy Lakhdar Brahimi, US Secretary of State John Kerry, Russia's Foreign Minister Sergei Lavrov, the men of the Opposition, the men of Assad's government, the men of the Iranian, Saudi, Turkish, and Qatari governments, the officers and conscripts in the Assad government military, the commanders and fighters for the Syrian anti-Assad militias, the commanders and fighters for the foreign Islamist militias.

While Syrian civil society activist women continued their embassy rounds, no official offered to do anything. They did not expend any of their own political capital to bring civil society activists into the negotiations. They did not even offer to get the women passes so they could get inside the negotiation building. Officials' meetings with these ten Syrian women representatives might merely have allowed their governments to claim that they "cared" about Syrian women without actually doing anything to ensure that their important voices—their knowledge, their peace strategies—were effectively heard inside the negotiating room.

As the official negotiations came unraveled, our alternative feminist meeting came to a close. We all returned to our local work. Remarkably, the Syrian civil society activist women packed up so they could travel back across boundaries, through checkpoints into the war zone. Their work was not done.

EPILOGUE: JANUARY 2017

The 2014 women activists' efforts to compel the UN Special Envoy for Syria and his US and Russian co-convenors to take seriously women's ideas about political solutions, experiences of war's violence, and proposals for post-war political, economic, and societal reconstruction seemed to fall on patriarchally deaf ears. Yet, it turned out, they were not without some effect.

By early 2016, with the Syrian war still raging and spilling over into neighboring Iraq and Turkey, and with the US government pouring resources, special forces, and air power into the conflict, while the Russian government was becoming a direct combatant on Assad's side via its air force, there were renewed efforts to find some narrow ground on which to restart peace talks.

The UN's Special Envoy for Syria had changed. Lakhdar Brahimi, who had displayed so little interest in including women civil society activists in the 2014 Geneva talks, had been replaced by the Italian Swedish diplomat Staffan de Mistura, who seemed more open to the genuine participation of women. In February 2016, de Mistura announced the creation of a Syrian Women's Advisory Board. Its twelve members were to advise him as he engaged with the official negotiators for the Assad regime and the Opposition. UN Women greeted the creation of the Advisory Board as a substantial step forward in making Syrian civil society women activists' voices heard. Some of the activists themselves— as well as their transnational feminist allies in WILPF, ICAN, and Kvinna till Kvinna—were encouraged by this new development, though they were not sanguine. Mouna Ghanem of the Syrian Women's Forum for Peace joined the Advisory Board, but with her eyes wide open. After all, civil society women were still two handshakes away from actual negotiations, as stop-and-go as those inconclusive talks were. Everything would depend on de Mistura forcefully carrying their messages into the room, and on the rival male negotiators taking those messages seriously.

There was a second cause for caution. The UN Special Envoy insisted that women representing the Assad regime have places on the Advisory Board. Moreover, he told the dozen diverse women selected that they would have to come up with a shared list of demands. That is, while the masculinized negotiating teams inside the room would continue to face off against each other as presumed rivals, women on the Advisory Board, though they represented equally opposed political constituencies, would be taken seriously only if they somehow managed to reach a consensus.

As always, women trying to get their feet in the door of a masculinized decision-making process would have to weigh whether an opening offered by the men inside was a genuine opportunity or just window-dressing. As thousands fled Aleppo, and as women and girls already in refugee camps tried to challenge girls' early marriages, Syrian activist women inside and outside the war-torn country were asking whether this latest offer was genuinely transformative. It was possible that the new UN-devised Syrian Women's Advisory Board did not represent a meaningful rollback of international patriarchy. Instead, it might be the masculinized international system's latest adaptation in a long line of innovations designed to sustain patriarchy's core.

In December of 2016, ignoring the UN, as well as the US and British diplomats, Russian, Turkish, and Syrian political elites reached their own short-lived ceasefire agreement for Aleppo. It brought an end to Russian aerial bombing, which in turn allowed Aleppo's remaining civilians and Opposition fighters to flee, which, in turn, enabled the Assad's regime's military forces to exert control over the entire city. As patriarchal as the United Nations system continues to be, it did not hold a patriarchal candle to this Russian, Turkish, and Syrian regime trio.

So here we have one current model for sustaining patriarchy.

First, exclude women from the serious business of ending an armed violence.

Secondly, when begrudgingly accepting some women's participation, keep them on the fringes of the final decision-making.

Thirdly, make such demands on those allegedly fortunate women allowed on to the fringes of serious decision-making that their own fragile alliances are frayed.

Fourthly, while the diplomatic negotiations stumble along, go ahead with the masculinized armed violence, thereby perpetuating the patriarchal notion that aerial bombing and "boots on the ground" will be the ultimate decider of who wins the war.

Spelling out this model for wrong-headed "sustainability" may make it seem all the more impossible to effectively challenge patriarchal ways of conducting what passes for international affairs. That is not quite true, however. Seeing each step followed by the next may be discouraging, but it is revealing. It pulls back the camouflaged cover on patriarchal politics. It shows it to be not the inevitable (read: unaccountable) workings of the unseen hand of history. Rather, laying it out like this shows such a patriarchal scenario to be deliberately scripted. In so exposing it, feminists can challenge it, and hold all parties accountable, every step of the way.

CHAPTER THREE

When Carmen Miranda Returns

It can be easy to slip into the sanguine notion that time itself creates positive change. *Back then*, systematic rape wasn't considered a war crime. *Back then*, women journalists were relegated to the paper's Style page. *Back then*, factory bosses could lock garment workers inside their unsafe factories. Phrasing it this way makes each change appear as though it didn't take analyzing, organizing and risk-taking by scores of diverse women and their male allies in scores of different societies to achieve even small advances. All it took to roll back patriarchy was the mere passage of time.

It is perhaps this optimism—a faith in the passage of time to create progress—that fueled my own too-easy presumption in 2013 that, after two decades of directing my attention elsewhere, when I revisited arenas in the globalized political economy I would find patriarchy in retreat.

I was in for a surprise.

Patriarchy is not reliant on just one or two attitudes that feminists have needed to challenge—for instance, that daughters are worth less parental investment than sons, or that men make better scientists than women—though, of course, those attitudes do indeed have to be altered if patriarchy is to be dismantled. Patriarchy is not even reliant on just a few relationships that feminists have had to transform—for example, men being given unlimited sexual access to their wives; or women being positioned in organizations as the loyal assistants to their male bosses. Though, again, transforming these patriarchal relationships has been a monumental task, which so many advocates of women's rights have taken on their shoulders. Patriarchy is a particular complex web of both attitudes and relationships that position women and men, girls and boys in distinct and unequal categories, that value particular forms of masculinity over virtually all forms of femininity, and—and this is crucial—that ensure that men who fulfill these favored forms of manliness will be able to assert control over most women.

In other words, patriarchy is wide and it is deep. It is distinct, but it feeds off both racism and classism.

Patriarchy's workings are not automatically rejected by women and girls. There are many rewards bestowed on a woman who finds ways to fit into a patriarchal system: marital economic security, societal respectability; even, occasionally, state honors. The woman who does not rebel against patriarchy will be complimented on her beauty, on her femininity, on her loyalty (as a daughter, a wife, a secretary); she will be praised for her endurance, her good sense, her domestic skills, her maternal devotion, her sexual appeal, her caring sacrifice, her patriotism.

Patriarchy, precisely because it is woven out of so many ideas and sustained through such a plethora of intimate and formal relationships, is stubborn, while also surprisingly flexible.

I have the original Hollywood poster here in my study. It was my brother, David, a 1940s movie buff, who found it. The poster announced Busby Berkeley's 1943 film *The Gang's All Here*. It was one of his over-the-top cinematic extravaganzas. Its release came during a brutalizing wartime. Most moviegoers were just clawing their way out of a deep economic depression. But in Busby Berkeley's world it was all giant strawberries.

David had hunted down the poster because he knew that I had become suddenly intrigued by the political roles played by the Brazilian actress and singer Carmen Miranda. By 1943 she had left Brazil, where she had become a radio and recording star, to dazzle audiences first on Broadway stages and then on Hollywood's silver screen. Technicolor was made for her. There she is in the middle of the movie poster, strutting between phalanxes of giant strawberries. On her head is a plantation's worth of bananas. This was the striking image splashed across the cover of *Bananas, Beaches and Bases*, where I started my journey to make feminist sense of international politics.

I began doing the research that led to *Bananas, Beaches and Bases* in the late 1980s, after having already spent more than a decade investigating and teaching about racism in militaries, the comparative politics of women, and the politics of Southeast Asia. I wrote the manuscript specifically for the innovative small British feminist publisher Pandora Press. A year after its British publication (in 1989), *Bananas* was published in the United States, by the University of California Press. While I consciously wrote the book for a feminist trade press, it was after its publication in paperback by a well-known university press that it seemed to take off. Frankly, that took me by surprise.

Looking back, I realize that it was the timing that was propitious. In the early 1990s, more women's studies teachers were trying to internationalize their courses. Simultaneously, more teachers of international politics were beginning to explore the long-ignored gendered dynamics of those relationships.

Bananas. It had taken me a surprisingly long time to think about bananas politically and internationally, and an even longer time to ask where were the women (and thus where were the men) in the global politics of bananas—and why? I say "surprising" because, for years, I had been in close proximity to other plantation crops. In Malaysia I had lived on the edge of a rubber plantation. In the coolness of the tropical mornings, I would watch the Malaysian Indian tappers as they emptied the latex-filled coconut cups tacked to the slim, dappled rubber trees. Just a few years earlier, Communist guerrillas had controlled this plantation, but by the mid-60s the latex was once again flowing and heading for the international market, where it would be turned by Dunlop into tennis balls and automobile tires.

Five years later I was teaching a night-time class for a group of civil servants at Guyana's national university. The campus was situated on the fringe of a sugar plantation. Large beetles flew through the open windows of our classroom, attracted by the light. This was in post-colonial Guyana. The multinational corporation Booker still owned most of Guyana's sugar, though it was Guyanese Indian workers who performed the hard work of planting and harvesting the cane.

Rubber and sugar. Tappers and cane workers. Dunlop and Booker. Malaysia and Guyana. For years, I thought about all of them without any gender curiosity. Race, ethnicity, class, nationality—those were the concepts that provided me with my analytical lenses. Each concept was—and has remained—crucial for making sense of the politics of rubber and sugar. Imagining plantation workers anywhere simply as "workers" will not yield reliable political explanations, much less forecasts. Yet, even when combined, these four complicating and clarifying concepts have turned out to be inadequate to explain the full workings of power that made and still make (and occasionally transform) the international politics of globalized plantation crops: rubber and sugar, as well as coffee, tea, pineapples, and palm oil.

When I returned twenty years later to international banana politics as I was writing a revised and updated *Bananas, Beaches and Bases*, some of the political players were strikingly the same: Chiquita (formerly United Fruit), Dole and Del Monte; the government officials of the United States, the Philippines, the United Kingdom, Costa Rica, Nicaragua, Colombia, and the Windward Islands; housewife consumers; banana workers' unions. But I soon discovered that there were also new actors claiming roles on bananas' world stage: large globalized supermarket chains such as Carrefour, Tesco, Walmart, and Costco; the ambitious Ecuadorian anti-union banana magnate Álvaro Noboa and his Bonita brand; the World Trade Organization (WTO); Brussels-based EU officials; fairtrade non-governmental organizations (NGOs); the transnational network of women banana workers. And, of course, the electronic social media: it has connected plantation worker activists and food security activists. The Web, however, has also reduced Carmen Miranda to merely an inspiration for drag selfies.

Despite all these changes, I discovered that two things have persisted. First, as in earlier decades, today's international political economy of bananas would have come unraveled without the labor of low-paid and unpaid women. This sophisticated system of growing and shipping and marketing a fragile fruit has been made to rely on imagining that women's work is unskilled and that their wages are mere "pin money." Secondly, even with this being the reality, and even with the recent outpourings of smart feminist-informed scholarly studies and activist reporting, it remains all too easy for many (most?) international political commentators to dismiss gender investigations of a highly profitable globalized product as an analytical sideshow. This is worth thinking about next time you slice a banana on top of your morning cereal.

The workings of globalizing patriarchy, which had been so often trivialized in the late twentieth century, I found still remained an afterthought for many observers, even critical observers, who claimed to make sense of the world today. It was not just patriarchy that had proved sustainable, it was many experts' lack of feminist curiosity that had persisted. Who is making the gender analysis of the World Trade Organization a featured case study in their university lectures? Which teachers are encouraging their students to undertake explicitly gendered analyses of the international politics of Tesco, Carrefour, or Chiquita? If anyone in a university, in an agency, or in a large NGO answers such a question confidently with, "Oh, our gender specialist handles those things," that is evidence of the persistent "sideshow" phenomenon. Paying close attention to what is getting relegated to a "sideshow"—and who exactly is doing the relegating—can shine a bright light on what it is taking to sustain patriarchy.

By doing a "gender analysis" I mean, initially, charting over time the positions of the women and of the men on all rungs on the ladder of any organization, institution, industry, or social movement. Then, looking at the chart, one needs to discover how the women got some places, and the men got other places.

Next question to pose: who benefits from most women and men being where they are? "Gendering," in other words, does not happen just down on the lowest rungs—in the trenches, on the assembly floor, amid the rubber trees, in the voting booths. Gendering happens up on the elite rungs as well. If most of those who are involved in trade treaty bargaining (or in peace negotiating or *coup d'état* plotting) are men, that decision-making is usually riddled with the workings of manliness. For instance, in each process there are likely to be efforts by one of the participants, maybe most of them, to feminize the others in order to damage their credibility.

Therefore, doing a gender analysis also requires that one investigate (again, over time) each and every manipulation—by any of the actors, whether rivals or allies—of the ideas and practices of both masculinities and femininities. For example, when the male executives running the big three banana corporations introduced washing-sheds on their plantations in the 1960s, they manipulated ideas about femininity and what it meant to do "women's work." They engaged in these sorts of patriarchal manipulations so that they could justify characterizing washing-shed work as low-skilled precisely because women were performing it. Women wash. That is what women do naturally. Thus it is not a skill. Therefore, it does not have to be paid for as if it were skilled work.

Similarly, ideas about manliness are manipulated for organizational objectives. When the men (and occasionally a few women) devise strategies to recruit sufficient numbers of young men into either their statist or insurgent armed forces, they routinely portray fighting—or at least their wielding of weapons—as proving "real" manhood. If they can convince enough young men of the authenticity of this gender credential, they will be able, they believe, to fill their militarized ranks.

Doing gender analysis is intellectually demanding. Neither casual observations nor stereotypical assumptions are enough. I learned this anew as I set about writing the updated *Bananas, Beaches and Bases.* Yet, when I plunged into the updating of the international politics of military bases, of bananas, of garments, of tourism, of diplomacy, of domestic workers, and of nationalism, I was struck again by how, amidst all the admittedly important changes that had occurred during that last twenty-five years, the patriarchal dynamics of international politics had persisted.

Finding these persistencies has reinforced my sense that patriarchy is a crucial concept for making reliable sense of international politics. It is not some old-fashioned notion. Patriarchy is as up-to-date as the ripest banana and as the deadliest military unit.

International political relationships and tendencies are patriarchal when either of them depends, in significant measure, on the privileging of certain sorts of masculinities in both the distributions of power and the distributions of status and material rewards. And patriarchy is at work when anything that is deemed feminine is positioned either on a pedestal, to be admired but not to wield authority, or on the lower rungs of the international system's ranked order, where it can be controlled and/or exploited for the benefit of those deemed less feminized.

At the same time, finding these persistencies has made me newly aware of international political patriarchy's remarkable capacities for adaptation. The only way to study adaptability is to track the phenomenon over time. Merely to pay attention to the present will lead one to underestimate the capacities of any structural system, or of any cultural system, for adaptation. And that will risk not only failing to press for meaningful change, but being left in the theoretical dust.

Here are some patriarchal persistencies I uncovered while researching the new edition of *Bananas, Beaches and Bases*.

The Pentagon can close its mammoth Subic navy base in the Philippines, and dramatically expand its bases in Guam and Italy, and open new "lily pad" bases in the United Arab Emirates and Sub-Saharan Africa, yet the US security doctrine continues to depend on government-to-government agreements to control the interactions of local women with its own male military personnel. Look at any government's military bases anywhere on the globe. Each of those military bases—American, Russian, Chinese, French, British, Saudi—depends in part on governments controlling soldier husbands' relationships with their civilian wives, who usually are left back at home (see Chapter Six). Simultaneously, each of those bases relies on cooperating with host government officials to regulate sexual relationships between military men (and militarized contractor men) and local or refugee girls and women in the vicinity.

Nationalists of assorted stripes may now be utilizing Facebook and Twitter, yet a great many of them continue to envision an old-fashioned "nation" made up of masculinized protectors and the feminized protected. In that sort of nation, the protectors remain the ones popularly presumed to have the skills required to lead peace negotiations, write constitutions, rank state priorities, deploy security forces, and go head-to-head with foreign rivals.

Foreign service bureaucracies of myriad countries can open their diplomatic career tracks to more women and even declare that diplomats' spouses need only perform social roles as "volunteers"; nonetheless, they can continue to rely on women as unpaid wives to grease the diplomatic gears of their trade and security negotiations. (The growing numbers of diplomatic spouses who are male do not really figure into this persistent calculation.)

Globalized apparel corporations can migrate from South Korea to China, or to Bangladesh, Indonesia, or Cambodia, while also inserting more intermediaries between themselves and the workers at the sewing machines, with the goal of staving off the criticisms of new NGO monitors; all the while, those same corporations' executives and their host country state elite partners persist in masculinizing their own alliances and in feminizing clothing production as the joint *sine qua non* of their respective institutional securities. Mango, North Face, and Old Navy may offer hip new styles, but they are relying on old gender formulas.

Now, a warning: to uncover these continuities does not mean that nothing in the gendered character of international politics has changed in recent decades. In fact, each of these explorations has shown me how much more work—how many more exercises of power—it takes now than it did, say, in the 1980s to sustain international patriarchal cultures and structures.

Those women who today are challenging the privileging of certain forms of masculinity and the "cheapening" of certain forms of femininity have garnered new resources and crafted new analytical concepts with which to both shed a bright light on, and disrupt, globalized patriarchal operations—in political economy and in security. For instance, transnational feminist activists from dozens of groups have created networks such as the NGO Working Group on Women, Peace and Security. Based in New York, this transnational network closely monitors efforts by states and lobbying groups to roll back women's rights and dilute gender equity commitments made by the UN Secretariat and UN member states. The NGO Working Group's meticulously savvy monitoring does not mean that those subversive patriarchal efforts do not persist; but today they are less able to pass unnoticed. This, in turn, means that both UN and member state officials now have to spend more energy and political currency trying to explain away their complicity with efforts to sustain patriarchy.

Or consider the international patriarchal politics of domestic workers, 80 percent of whom are women. Over the last twenty years, more and more states have become dependent for their economic wellbeing on remittances sent home by women working abroad as migrant domestic workers: the Philippines, Sri Lanka, Indonesia, Brazil, Peru, and Jamaica. At the same time, more state elites of the importing countries—Jordan, Singapore, Hong Kong, Malaysia, Qatar—have made the importation of women to clean the private homes of their expanding middle classes evidence that they have entered the exclusive club of modern societies.

Yet, while overcoming formidable obstacles, such as intimidation by host governments and by their own home governments' reluctance to do anything to jeopardize the uninterrupted flow of remittances from their women overseas, domestic workers themselves have fashioned new concepts of work and a transnational organization, the International Domestic Workers Federation (IDWF) to wield that concept. In 2011, the IDWF's activists succeeded, against all odds, in persuading the state delegates gathered in Geneva at the headquarters of the International Labour Organization (ILO) to pass ILO Convention 189 (C189), the world's first international treaty explicitly guaranteeing the labor rights of women and men employed as domestic workers.

The fact that ILO C189 is a historic first is testimony to how many forms of power have been wielded to keep domestic workers' labor conditions privatized, to keep domestic work immune from international protections. Privatization, of course, is a political process—both a national and an international one. It has taken decades of strategizing and action to keep that immunity in place. Patriarchy's sustainability is itself a process, requiring thought, actions, and alliance-making. Ensuring, decade after decade, that there is an ideological melding of the private, the domestic, and the feminine has been central to the perpetuation of patriarchal politics of paid domestic work nationally and internationally.

This makes domestic workers' success in creating the IDWF, and in winning the passage of ILO C189, all the more notable. Patriarchal sustainability is not unstoppable. Nonetheless, both achievements do not mean that Filipina, Sri Lankan, Indonesian, Jamaican, Peruvian, and Brazilian domestic workers can now keep their own passports when they take a job in Jordan or Singapore; these achievements alone do not guarantee that most national legislatures will soon ratify C189. Among those governments that have refused are the United Kingdom and the United States. According to the IDWF's own website, by October

2016, five years after the victory in Geneva, only twenty-three governments had ratified the Convention.

On October 11, after their government ratified C189, women activists in the Jamaica Household Workers' Union posed for a celebratory photo. Each woman wore a blue T-shirt inscribed with the radical assertion: "Domestic Work Is Work."

Sustainable patriarchy continues to nurture the myth that a home is a private place beyond the reach of human rights laws. The corollary is that work performed inside that private place is not "real" work. The same assertion that continues to make recognizing and prosecuting domestic violence difficult also makes it challenging to recognize domestic workers as workers. The formation of the IDWF and the passage of ILO Convention 189 have not relegated these complementary myths to the attic, but they have meant that today, just as with the UN, it is taking more energy, and more political currency, for those who benefit from the politicized notion of feminized domestic work to perpetuate those patriarchal ideas, and to hold on to the benefits that flow from them.

During these recent reflections I've been reminded how helpful it is to write wearing my teaching hat. I think of teaching in its broadest sense. It is a strategy that is useful not simply when one is writing for readers who are reading as students, but also when writing for peers and colleagues. Writing with one's teaching hat on strengthens analytical writing because it encourages one to imagine (and respect) the eventual readers. Teaching becomes more effective when one keeps an eye not on the lecture notes but on the students. Over the years, a teacher becomes attuned to the subtle (well, sometimes not-so-subtle) signals students send to express their skepticism: the back-row choice of seat, the raised eyebrow, the slumped posture, the notes passed to a neighbor— and the ubiquitous laptop opened to Facebook.

Thank goodness. Such telltale gestures signal that the point one is trying to get across is stuck midstream, that an alternative communication tack should be tried. These signals are sent regularly to teachers who have become convinced that adopting an explicit gender analysis is crucial to making reliable sense of international politics. It is at this juncture that a gender-alert teacher has to demonstrate that if her or his listeners fail to take seriously the political workings of femininities and masculinities they will devise explanations of the world they live in that are not merely incomplete—we all live with incompletion—but unreliable.

In other words, when doing either analytical teaching or writing for any audience, one needs to respect readers' and listeners' skepticism—not a skepticism that flows from arrogance or gamesmanship; rather, a skepticism that derives from a genuine inability to see the relevance of an unfamiliar line of investigation. Students want to know—and deserve to know—why any newly introduced idea or fresh line of questioning matters. In this sense, they are inclined toward intellectual efficiency. They want to know—and deserve to know—what they will miss if they ignore a certain unfamiliar analytical pathway, and the price they will eventually pay if they continue to travel along the well-worn conventional highway, eschewing the extra work it will take to make their way down the rough-hewn new route.

So what will we miss if we continue to refuse to ask these sorts of feminist analytical questions? And how will missing it make the entire explanation being offered untrustworthy?

I have been thinking about respect for authentic skepticism as I have returned to the international politics of bananas—and of bases, beaches, domestic work, diplomacy, and nationalism. While more listeners and readers today at least recognize a teaching and research field called "Gender and International Relations," and may even have read one or two articles by analysts who employ feminist investigatory concepts, gender curiosity continues to be treated as marginal and therefore optional in the majority of international political inquiries. Thus the questions *What will I miss?* and *Why does it matter?* still resonate.

Having revisited the specific gender-political dynamics that shape international phenomena as apparently disparate as military base doctrine, nationalist movements and the political economies of food, apparel, hotels, and scrubbing the tub, I think that I am more equipped now to address both of these useful questions.

What will one miss if one does not take seriously the workings of masculinities and femininities in international politics? Most significantly, I think, one will underestimate power. By ignoring (or politely giving merely a token nod to) feminist-informed gender analysis, one will grossly underestimate the range of sites and types of power, as well as the amounts of power that have been (and currently are) wielded in any process of creating and perpetuating the structures and belief systems that prop up the complex patriarchal international political system. Many "mainstream" international commentators leave uninvestigated and unaccounted-for the kinds of power and the repeated uses of power by state officials trying to control women's relations with the state and women's relationships with diverse men. These analysts do not track the genderings—and re-genderings—of the international politics of marriage, of labor, of citizenship and migration, of trade, of debt, of militarism and armed conflict, of international organizations, of state-building, and of post-war state rebuilding.

This lack of curiosity is easier to sustain if one does not take women—all kinds of women, not all heroic, not all admirable — seriously. If one lumps "child soldiers" together, "insurgents" together, "civil society" together, if one refers to "Russia" or "China" as monolithic state actors, it is easier to deny the impacts that the politics of masculinities and femininities have on each of those actors and on the relationships between them. Similarly, if one treats Walmart, Apple, Fox News, Twitter, Mango, Hyundai, Tesco, BAE Systems, or Foxconn as unified, ungendered decision-makers, then it is easier to ignore the constant workings of masculinities and femininities that determine who exactly makes the international decisions in the name of each of these entities.

Asking *Where are the women?* is a shorthand for investigating where the women are (by class, nationality, sexuality, race) in any organization or in any state, and where the men (by class, nationality, sexuality, race)—and why. Disaggregating any international actor intersectionally by gender, of course, does make one's analytical job more taxing. One has to become more curious about the internal dynamics of any presumably unified actor. One of the most valuable contributions of feminist-informed international analysts has been their revealing how intra-organizational gender dynamics affect both inter-state and intra-state, as well as intra-corporate, dynamics. The UN Security Council, the US State Department, the Turkish military, the Chinese Politboro—we currently know almost nothing about the workings of masculinities and of femininities inside any of these influential organizations. Underestimating actors in international politics, combined with underestimating power, its myriad deployments and the repeated challenges to those deployments, is a significant outcome of not honing and using gender-analytical skills.

When one begins to take into account the full range of and wieldings of power, one is more able to see that patriarchal cultures and structures are not natural. They are not automatically sustainable. Instead, they are devised and constantly refined. Daily. They are challenged and defended. Hourly.

Thanks to advances in political theorizing, we know this about states. We know this about capitalist cultures and structures. We know this about regimes or racist systems. But many of us still do not want to recognize this about the cultures and structures that perpetuate distinctively gendered international relationships.

Why does the missing of this in this way matter? This is the second question that is rightly posed by the authentically skeptical listeners and readers. It matters because, collectively, we are investing so much energy into reducing inequities, redressing injustices, assuring rights, and ending violence. I have become increasingly convinced that if we devise even well-intentioned solutions without paying serious attention to how ideas about and practices of manliness and of femininities flourish, our solutions will be short-lived and woefully inadequate.

One reason that both old-fashioned and updated patriarchies are not topics at most bargaining tables is because no one who is invited to sit at the solution-devising table is equipped with the sophisticated analytical feminist skills to know what to do with gender if, by some chance, patriarchy did make it on to the agenda. Feminism is a combination of particular values and commitments. But it also is a set of distinctive skills, investigatory skills, explanatory skills. The skills necessary to weigh the causes and consequences of the politics of masculinities and femininities are stunningly absent among most people invited to sit at such high tables. In their stead are the tools wielded to sustain patriarchy: casual essentialisms, parochial analogies, ill-informed guesses, misogynist fears, and dismissive jokes.

Those practices may not look like tools. In fact, their very effectiveness depends on their not looking like tools. But they are. They are tools designed to perpetuate patriarchy. They are not designed to transform today's international political system in ways that provide dignity, opportunity and genuine security to most of this planet's citizens.

CHAPTER FOUR

Tourism and Complicity at Ticonderoga, Gettysburg, and Hiroshima

My father had come home from the Indian, Burmese, British, and German war zones of World War II. My mother, who had spent most of the war as a *de facto* single mother, supplied solace for my father as he bumpily re-entered civilian life. It was post-war peacetime, a time when my parents could take my brother and me on modest vacations. They both liked road trips. One of the family expeditions I most vividly remember was to the shores of Lake Champlain in upstate New York. The high point of the trip was a visit to Fort Ticonderoga. I must have been about ten years old. Just learning how to say "Ticonderoga" seemed like an adventure.

The fort was built on a contested strategic site in 1755, when French and English colonial troops fought each other for control of what were then forested frontier regions, crisscrossed by valuable lake and river trade routes. Each warring European power had its own Native American allies. The fort became more famous several decades later as a battle site during the early years of the American Revolutionary War. In 1775 the heralded Green Mountain Boys of rebellious Vermont crossed the lake to seize the fort from the British. Even in the early days of the Republic, the fort thereafter was deemed to be of historic value, worthy of preservation. Initially it was the property of the state of New York, then was owned and turned into a museum by a wealthy New York merchant family, and finally taken over by the federal government, which declared the fort a National Historic Landmark.[1]

At the time my mother and father took my brother and me there, "Fort Ti" had become a popular destination for local tourists. It combined a romanticized American history narrative with a beautiful geographic site. I already would have known something about the American Revolution from my public elementary school history lessons. My teachers, however, would not have guided my schoolmates and me through the murkier politics of the preceding "French and Indian War" and certainly would not have given us insight into the tough strategic calculations each Native American tribe had had to make during both of these late-eighteenth-century armed conflicts.

Surprisingly, looking back on this childhood visit to a military fort and battle site, what I most clearly remember are not the cannons or the beautiful lake views from atop the battlements, but the interior museum displays—especially the uniforms. There were wool, slightly moth-eaten but still distinctly red jackets fitted on headless mannequins. Every American child knew about "the redcoats." What struck ten-year-old me, though, was how short these British red-jacketed soldiers must have been. I think that I even exclaimed to my mother at these military men's short stature. They didn't seem to be much taller than me. I learned something that day that, on the face of it, doesn't seem particularly militarized: that the average heights of people of seemingly the same national/racial "stock" could change dramatically over the centuries.

Perhaps because Fort Ticonderoga's restoration and museum then featured no battle re-enactments and no paintings of bloody engagements, I didn't come away from this early tourist adventure with any sense of violence, pain, or loss. I did absorb a sense of wartime victory, but it was rather vague. Perhaps that made its absorption all the more insidious. What I remembered best was that short male soldier's faded red jacket.

Becoming a feminist makes one more reflective. That, of course, can be uncomfortable. When I first began investigating both the surface and subterranean processes by which women and men—and their gendered communities, workplaces, entertainments, and governments—become militarized, I had to think about the dynamics of my own girlhood and, even more discomfitingly, those of my parents' marriage. I read my mother's diary with fresh eyes. I thought anew about how my father's military participation in World War II affected their relationship. I began then to see that the US government depended on my mother for its waging of that globalized war.

That is what becoming a feminist investigator of militarization does: it makes large militarizing structures and cultural tendencies clearer, while shining a bright light on complicities closer to home that sustain those apparently distant systems.

By complicity, I mean lending one's moral or behavioral support to any institution's legitimacy, effectiveness, and credibility, without speaking out directly in favor of, or taking explicit actions to contribute to that support. In this sense, complicity is a sort of "stealth support."

When being complicit, the contributor remains seemingly innocent or uninvolved. Consequently, complicity in any process of militarization can feel rather comfortable. Comfortable, that is, until one is pushed to develop a feminist consciousness and a more energetically reflective curiosity. The camouflaging curtain of innocence and non-involvement is jerked away. At that point, one's former complicity is harder to deny.

Thus it is only now, rather belatedly, that I have begun to think back on my own experiences of militarized tourism. That may seem odd. After all, I've been digging into gendered militarization since the early 1980s. Yet that may be precisely the point: the processes of gendered militarization are so subtle, so disparate, and many of the sites where it occurs so seemingly peaceful, that I am now, decades later, still discovering new personal experiences on which to throw a feminist beam of discomfiting analytical light.

Before I ever thought back reflectively on that childhood visit with my parents to "Fort Ti," I focused my attention on a form of militarized tourism that was more obvious: the tourism of male soldiers in the midst of a war. I was doing this early research in the 1980s, in the aftermath of the US-Vietnam war. What caught my attention then was what American male soldiers did on leave. Still very new to crafting a feminist curiosity, I started to track American male soldiers who were taking "rest and recreation" in Bangkok. I tried to find out how their pursuit of pleasure fueled the Thai prostitution industry. I looked at Thai government officials' masculinized responses to the influx of American soldiers in search of sexualized entertainment. And I thought about the Thai women who provided that entertainment. Bangkok, then, was my first site for analyzing gendered militarized tourism. Bangkok was far away from upstate New York. Its dynamics seemed so far removed from a family outing that I didn't even try to make the connections between male soldiers in a wartime brothel and civilians enjoying a lakeside tourist attraction. In not making those connections, I left my own complicity comfortably unexamined.

My complicity in militarized tourism extended into young adulthood. Having come of age in California in the early twentieth century, my mother was a genuine "roadie." She loved driving. Together, we drove across Canada (in a VW Bug), across the American Southwest (in a VW station wagon), and from Rome to Paris (in a little Fiat). Most of our driving trips, however, took us up and down the American East Coast. We both loved staying at old inns and stopping at historical sites. During one summer break while I was in graduate school, we decided to explore central Pennsylvania. We chose Gettysburg as one of our destinations.

This was in the mid-1960s. Civil War memory was not as saturated with novels, re-enactments, Hollywood movies, and filmed documentaries as it has since become. African American critical historiography of slavery and the abolitionist movement was just beginning to blossom. Studies by feminist historians of white and black women's Civil War experiences (and their distinct contributions to anti-slavery movements) were just coming into print. Still, "Gettysburg" already had taken root in the collective American consciousness. Thanks in large measure to President Abraham Lincoln's eloquent battlefield eulogy delivered there in 1864, "Gettysburg" evoked wartime sorrow.

Being a tourist at Gettysburg seemed emotionally quite different from being a tourist at Fort Ticonderoga. My mother and I felt it; we absorbed the distinctive Gettysburg mood. As we walked across the rolling green fields where the July 1863 battle took place between male soldiers of the Union and the Confederacy, we became solemn. In just three days, 51,112 soldiers had died, been injured, captured, or gone missing.[2]

There were signposts on the battlefield telling us where Lee's soldiers were, where Grant's troops were, who advanced or retreated when. But neither my mother nor I was enticed to trace these battle logistics. We had seen some of Mathew Brady's grainy black and white battlefield photographs. We knew that the bodies of men dead and dying were once strewn across these now-beautiful green fields. I don't know if, as we walked, my mother thought of my father's own wartime doctoring or of the grieving mothers of sons killed here.[3] Although my mother and I were "Northerners," white Northerners, by heritage, I don't recall either of us expressing the least sense of being at a site of victory for "our side."

Today I wonder how gendered are the experiences of being a civilian battlefield tourist. For instance, in any given year—then or now—are disproportionately more male than female tourists likely to take the initiative to follow the National Park Service's signposts to track the Union's and Confederacy's military maneuvers? And which souvenirs in the large Gettysburg battlefield gift shop are young boys most likely to purchase? I wonder if their souvenir-buying patterns are any different from those of their sisters. Maybe little girl tourists are more drawn to the books about those women who traveled to wartime Gettysburg to serve as volunteer nurses. And what about African American boys and girls? To make full sense of the workings of today's militarized tourism, one has to be curious about their experiences of Gettysburg, their own distinctive emotions and attractions. Then there is the gendering of parenting among militarized tourist site visits. One can employ a feminist curiosity to explore what "lessons" fathers and mothers of each nationality and race pass along to their sons and to their daughters on such battlefield family outings.

Sorrow and solemnity: I now wonder how they too can be militarized. I may have imagined back then, when I first visited Gettysburg, that the sorrow I felt while walking across a deceptively peaceful former battlefield a century after the gun smoke had blown away and the carnage had been carted off was a demilitarized emotion. But that would be true only if the sorrow I felt did not grow out of my unconscious presumption that fallen young men dying as soldiers were worthy of more emotional investment than, say, young male migrants dying when their leaky boats sank at sea, or middle-aged women dying, one by one, at the hands of their violent male domestic partners.

My visit to Hiroshima came several decades after my mother's and my Gettysburg visit. By then, I had spent years researching the myriad forms that the militarizations of masculinities and of femininities can take. So I visited Hiroshima equipped with a heightened consciousness. Thanks to feminism, I was more reflective, less innocent. I was on guard, newly aware of how civilians on holiday were gendered, usually patriarchally gendered, and how they could become militarized—and nurture militarization. By the time I visited Hiroshima, therefore, friends and colleagues had made me more wary of my own complicity in gendered militarism.

I was in Japan serving as a guest lecturer in Tokyo at the famous women's university, Ochanomizu. When I told my Japanese feminist friends that I was planning a train trip to Kyoto and Hiroshima, they offered caveats. This was the early 2000s, when the US government under George W. Bush was exerting enormous pressure on Japanese officials to send troops, even if in token numbers, to support the US-led war effort in Iraq. Thousands of Japanese women and men came out into the streets to protest any Japanese military involvement in Iraq, however allegedly tokenist.

My Japanese feminist friends took me along with them to these anti-war marches. They also took me with them to Tokyo Women in Black's Friday night antimilitarism vigils in Shinjuku, the city's neon-lit shopping district. Some of the Tokyo Women in Black feminists were trying to make more visible the role of both the 1930s and the 1940s Japanese militarists' ideology of the "good wife", as well as many Japanese women's internalization of that wartime-gendered ideology, in order to warn Japanese women today not to slip into imagining that that devastating war had been the work only of men.

These Japanese feminists were collectively on high alert for any attempts by current officials to dilute Japan's post-World War II commitment to peace, especially any efforts to deny the Imperial Army's "comfort women" system of sexual slavery, or to weaken Article 9 of the Japanese Constitution, an article that pledged the Japanese not to engage in any military actions beyond strictly defined self-defense.[4] It called for daily vigilance.

Japan's World War II historiography was the arena in which many of these contests—between those committed to Japanese pacifism and those eager to remilitarize Japan in the name of regaining international stature—were waged. Today these contests among Japanese are fiercer than ever. But even twelve years ago they were intense. My Japanese anti-militarist activist friends, consequently, did not take lightly my proposed trip to Hiroshima. They warned me against becoming, unwittingly, complicit in local nationalists' efforts to remilitarize Japan. They worried, in other words, that as a tourist I would absorb a militarizing message in Hiroshima: that Japan was best remembered not as a perpetrator of military aggression but as a wartime victim. So, when I set off by train from Tokyo, I had been forewarned.

The Peace Park in Hiroshima is, like so many militarized tourist sites, a strangely quiet place. The park is on the edge of Hiroshima's bustling post-war commercial center and a short walk from the city's baseball stadium, home of the Hiroshima Carp.[5] But in August 1945, on the eve of the American atomic bomb attack, this area had been an urban neighborhood crowded with homes, shops, businesses, and schools. I tried to keep my Japanese feminist friends' warning in mind as I walked from place to place in the park, as I read the memorials, as I rang the large peace bell. But it was hard. I was there as an American. I read as many Japanese names on the small memorials as I could, one by one. Most were civilians; many were children on their way to school that fateful day. I felt it was my responsibility to grasp the enormity of what the US government had perpetrated in 1945 in the name of my security.

The Peace Park includes a large museum, the Hiroshima Peace Memorial Museum.[6] The museum has two quite distinct wings. The older wing features exhibits showing the city before, during, and immediately after the atomic bombing. In this wing, the museum's curators invite tourists, both Japanese and foreigners, to look directly at the destruction and unthinkable pain wrought by the use of such horrific weaponry. It is not easy. There are no paeans here to Japanese imperialism or to Japanese male soldiers' honor and bravery. This is a peace museum. Yet a visitor does come away from this wing overwhelmed by the sense of what ordinary Japanese citizens suffered.

There is, however, a second wing to the museum. It is newer. It seems to be informed by the concerns voiced by my Tokyo feminist friends. This wing's exhibits are far less dramatic. They do not provoke such a visceral response. They have been designed, nonetheless, by their Japanese curators with an apparently intense sense of purpose. This new wing features displays of the Hiroshima World War II navy base. They make clear that Hiroshima was not simply a "city of innocents"; it was the site of militarization—gendered militarization. I had the feeling that this new wing's intended audience was Japanese, perhaps especially Japanese students, who visit in large numbers every year.

The museum's two wings seem to be in conversation with each other. The older wing is saying: "We suffered horribly here; the atomic weapons dropped here were inhumane and should never be used by anyone ever again." The new wing replies: "Yes, that is true, but the banishing of war's inhumanity will come only when we all face up to our own complicity in militarism."

Today, anyone visiting Hiroshima and its memorials will need to be mindful of the historical context of their own tourism. They will be wartime memorial visitors at a time when the current Japanese ruling party, the Liberal Democrats (LDP), is making determined efforts to weaken Japan's "peace constitution," especially to dilute its famous Article 9, in the name of increasing Japan's international influence. When Japanese Prime Minister Shinzo Abe, leader of the LDP, paid a much-publicized visit to Hawaii's Pearl Harbor war memorial at the end of 2016, was he forswearing military aggression, or laying the groundwork for Japan's normalization in the form of remilitarization? The Japanese debated this question among themselves, while they also tried to make Americans aware that either intent was possible. For their part, Japanese feminists continue to stay vigilant. They continue to do their best to resist remilitarizing efforts by showing their fellow citizens how remilitarization serves to reinforce their country's still potent forces of patriarchy. Japanese feminists, with their historical perspective and their acute observation, can teach us all valuable skills useful in shriveling patriarchy.

Today and in the upcoming years there will be multiple commemorations of the US Civil War (1861–65), World War I (1914–18), and World War II (1938–45). Every commemoration is seen by many countries' tourism promoters, and by the travel industry as a whole, as an opportunity to attract paying visitors. For instance, in New Mexico, at the White Sands Missile Range, often referred to as the "Trinity Site," visitors were drawn to the place where the US government and its wartime scientists detonated the first atomic bomb in 1945. Within weeks, its successor had been loaded onto the Boeing B-29 bomber *Enola*

Gay (named for the pilot's mother) to be dropped on Hiroshima. The Trinity Site has joined Fort Ticonderoga on the list of National Historic Landmarks and has been opened to visitors by the federal government. In April 2015, on the seventieth anniversary of the first test, 5,534 visitors came to Trinity, including Boy Scout troops, classes on field trips, and families.[7] In the heterosexual family groups, was it the father or the mother who suggested visiting Trinity? Do Girl Scout troop leaders match their Boy Scout counterparts in imagining Trinity as an attractive destination for a children's field trip?

Across the Atlantic, London tourism promoters developed walking tours and special museum exhibits to mark another memorable moment in the ongoing history of wartime aerial bombing: the seventy-fifth anniversary of the German Luftwaffe's fifty-seven consecutive nights of bombing British cities. The massive bombing, which began on September 7, 1940, was called the "Blitzkrieg," the "lightning war." Britons commonly refer to it as "the Blitz." Many of the 2015 anniversary events of this bombing as experienced by civilians from below appeared far removed from the quiet, reflective mood evoked in Hiroshima. Despite a growing number of British critical historians who are revealing the British class inequities exposed by the bombing, most of the events had as their theme the "plucky" communal spirit of all the British who endured the bombing. Some of the planned events appeared almost light-hearted: for instance, the Imperial War Museum's exhibit "Fashion on the Ration," or an entertainment company's "Blitz Party," with its promises of experiencing "wartime revelry" in an "authentic air raid shelter."[8]

As I reflect on these past and current militarized tourist sites and the experiences they offer to the traveler, I hesitate to jump to the conclusion that simply visiting a site that has been developed with a militarized imagination inevitably militarizes the visitor. Women and men, girls and boys, bring their own understandings, their own motivations, even their own tastes and enthusiasms to any tourist site. A person visiting a militarized site is not automatically complicit in militarization.

What becomes useful, then, is to investigate the complex interactions between the battle site's memorialization funders, its managers, curators, guides, low-waged site workers, and the physical exhibits, the landscapes, and the diverse visitors over time. Those interactions will certainly be shaped in some crucial part by each actor's understandings of competing masculinities and femininities—those that are deemed admirable, those to be pitied, and those to be despised. Courage, cowardice, fear, horror, loss, regret, endurance, suffering, passivity, aggression, selfishness, compassion, excitement—every militarized site is laced with all of these. And each of these emotions also is gendered, not just in how that site came to be militarized, but also in how that site is experienced by visitors for generations after the violence it witnessed has receded.

Militarization, in all its myriad gendered forms, can be perpetuated, can even creep ahead apace, in the quietest and greenest of places.

Thus, over the years, I have learned that a feminist curiosity needs to be deployed wherever forts, battlefields, weaponry, or bombed-out buildings are being preserved for tourists like me.

Bloody battle sites have become magnets for today's tourists: the Somme, Gallipoli, Sarajevo, Belfast, Pearl Harbor, Algiers, the Plains of Abraham, the Ho Chi Minh Trail. The full list is long. Its very length makes clear that a scene of past violence can be made attractive to today's travelers pursuing peaceful pleasure. It is a transformational process that perpetuates patriarchal understandings about femininities and masculinities and about the unequal relations between them across generations. That is, patriarchal transformations of sites of masculinized violence into places of post-war tourism serve to keep all sorts of manly men in their allegedly rightful places, and diversely feminine women in their socially approved places. Simultaneously, such battlefield transformations reinforce the likelihood that men will remain remembered as the protectors of women, and, as a necessary complement, women will be remembered as the grateful memorializers of brave men. As with so many workings of sustainable patriarchy, the processes by which a battlefield is turned into a tourist site are subtle. After all, a battlefield-turned-tourist attraction can be experienced by both women and men not as sites of oppression or domination, but, rather, as sites of emotional enrichment.

And battlefields are not the only places where patriarchal ideas and relationships are sustained. Parlors, pubs, brothels, bureaucratic corridors, television newsrooms, software offices, the floors of factories, stock markets, and legislatures—each is as likely as a battlefield to serve the interests of those trying to sustain patriarchy. Each can be turned into a place where women learn to respect (and defer to) men for their allegedly superior intellect, strategic savvy, physical courage, or worldly knowledge. This means, though, that each place can be transformed into a place of feminist resistance. Where patriarchal ideas and relationships flourish, there is the possibility that they can shrivel. For such shrivelings to occur, however, we need to view each of these places with fresh feminist eyes.

CHAPTER FIVE

Patriarchal Forgetting at Gallipoli, the Somme, and The Hague

History is not just about "yesterday." It is about today—and tomorrow. How we craft our personal and our collective memories shapes how we imagine ourselves in the world today. That, in turn, will influence how we feel and act tomorrow. What counts as courage, what deserves contempt, for whom do we grieve, who are the we in "we"? Each is either reinforced or challenged by how and what we choose to remember. It is for this reason that feminists pay such close attention to what is commemorated—and in what way, and by whom.

This attentiveness inspires feminists today to keep re-examining the past. It is why feminist libraries, feminist archives, feminist museums, and feminist historians are each so central to current challenges to patriarchy. Archivists, librarians, curators, and historians keep asking: what have we missed? They prompt us to keep wondering about what we have been told as children was unimportant, not worth noticing, certainly not worth commemorating. Who has been left out of the parade? Whose house hasn't yet warranted a blue plaque?

From 2014 through to 2018, we have been encouraged to commemorate the "Great War"—what we now think of as World War I. Feminists in Turkey, Australia, and New Zealand have tried to awaken the rest of us to what actors, what lessons, what legacies we have overlooked or have grossly misunderstood.

The Battle of Gallipoli began on April 25, 1915. At stake was the British Royal Navy's control of the Dardanelles and, with it, access to Russia. The battle lasted five and a half bloody months. Still today, a century later, people speak simply of "Gallipoli," the way people also speak of Gettysburg, Normandy, and Dien Bien Phu. A single place name comes to stand, in the minds of millions of people, not only for a significant military engagement, but for a collective trauma and an alteration of popular consciousness.

By contrast, like so many others outside of Turkey, Britain, New Zealand, and Australia, I first imagined the terrible Battle of Gallipoli only years after the battle itself, when I saw the 1981 Australian feature film *Gallipoli*. This much-praised movie marked the global launch of the New Wave of late-twentieth-century Australian filmmaking. The filmmakers told their story of rural Australian men who were sent to their almost-certain deaths far from home by misguided British commanders during the Great War. The scenes and the narratives were new to most American viewers, who could scarcely find Turkey on a map, much less Gallipoli. For Australians and New Zealanders, on the other hand, the 1981 film retold the story they had grown up hearing in their schools and from their grandparents and national leaders: how the wrong-headed Winston Churchill and his British generals crassly used their colonies' young men as cannon fodder in defense of the Empire, how their wartime defeat on those beachheads aroused nationalist consciousness among Australians, and how British imperialism for ever after would be deeply tainted in the eyes of its subjects Down Under.

How we tell and retell stories determines whether we sustain or challenge patriarchy. How we choose today to commemorate past events either breathes new life into patriarchy or helps dismantle it. We have almost daily personal and collective choices to make about history and "History."

The story of Gallipoli on film, and in its Australian and British popular retellings, is told from the vantage point of the beaches at the bottom of the Gallipoli cliffs. It is a masculinized story of misguided male commanders and brave, innocent male soldiers. For the British and imperial forces, the defeat was a humiliating, demasculinizing loss. If women appear in this version of the story, they appear as grieving mothers, widows, and girlfriends. If they were grieving in Australia and New Zealand, then they would be prompted to transform their grief into nationalist, anti-imperialist anger at the injustice done to "their" ill-used men.

Today, in New Zealand and Australia, April 25, Anzac Day, is a day to remember the lesson learned a century ago: the necessity of rescuing national pride from the ashes of military defeat. Thus New Zealand's and Australia's contemporary feminist peace activists deliberately choose Anzac Day each year to call on their fellow citizens to demilitarize their national cultures, to re-imagine nationalism: to eschew militarized masculinized heroism and to reject militarized feminized sacrifice.

But that is the story as told from the beachhead. It was Turkish feminists who taught me more recently to consider how another official story was being told. In 2003, Ayşe Gül Altınay and a group of Turkish feminists from four cities took me on a tour of militarized sites. In each, the multiple legacies of World War I and its aftermath still were alive in competing (though unequal) historical narratives. In Ankara, the capital, my feminist host was Ilknur Üstün. She thought I would find especially interesting the Atatürk Memorial, called Anıtkabir in Turkish, dedicated to the life of a military man, Mustafa Kemal, later anointed "Atatürk," who is credited as the "Father of the Modern Turkish Nation." Inside the imposing buildings, the featured exhibit is a large-scale diorama portraying the 1915–16 Battle of Gallipoli.

This time the story of the battle is told from above. The artists position us, the viewers, atop the cliffs, looking down at the invading British and imperial troops and their impressive navies lying offshore. The narrative is not only the January 1916 victory achieved by the forces of a tottering Ottoman Empire. Rather, the diorama is designed to persuade us of the emergence, here on the cliffs of Gallipoli, of a new post-Ottoman Turkish republican unified nation. It is a nation being born out of military heroism. It is a nation whose visionary leadership is embodied by the hero of Gallipoli, the Turkish commander Mustafa Kemal.

The dramatic scene that is laid out in the diorama is populated chiefly by male soldiers. One has to look closely to see any women painted into the mural. But women are there. They are portrayed as village women serving bravely as suppliers of provisions to the embattled male Turkish troops. For Atatürk himself, as well as for his male political successors, it was crucial that women be included, even if rather peripherally, in their story of the birth of the post-Ottoman modern Turkish nation.

For much the same reason, as Turkish feminist scholars tell us today, it was crucial that women's suffrage be introduced in the early years of the new Turkish Republic, though with a catch: while women intellectuals in fact had been advocating for women's rights throughout the latter decades of the waning Ottoman Empire, women's right to vote, when it came, would be narrated by nationalists as a gift to Turkish women by the World War I military hero Atatürk.

Taking account of the multiple gendered stories of "Gallipoli" reminds us of several anti-patriarchal lessons to be garnered from feminist analyses of World War I. First, any war is in fact comprised of multiple wars. While some "theaters" of battle may gain prominence in the post-war tellings, they are not the totality of that war. This is as true of the Crimean War, the US Civil War, the Boer War, the Korean War, the 1980–88 Iran-Iraq War, and the current Syrian War, as it is of World War I. Absorbing this truth makes us all much more wary of imagining that we have exposed the full array of interconnected gendered legacies of any war until we have used our feminist curiosities to thoroughly investigate each of the micro-wars that have been waged within what we rather simplistically call by a single overarching name.

Secondly, listening to Turkish, New Zealand, Australian, and British feminist explorers of "Gallipoli" reminds us that conventional tellers of war stories usually squeeze women into their tales only as bit players or, when they do catch the spotlight, as actors supporting the creation or affirmation of a certain kind of—patriarchal—nation. Feminist explorers of wars are more likely to encourage their listeners to think of their mothers, aunts, and grandmothers as having played multiple, often contradictory roles in the militarized emergence of any "nation." These enquiries, and the myriad experiences and understandings they expose, have the effect of making the nation less homogeneous, less monolithic, and less naturally patriarchal than presently portrayed. That is a step in the right direction, the direction of complexity.

Thus today Australian and New Zealand peace activist feminists continue to dig into the patriarchal consequences of the ways that the Gallipoli story is told precisely because it has been fashioned into a key building block of their respective society's politics of nationalism, each of those nationalisms threaded with assumptions about honorable masculinities and honorable femininities. Likewise, during centenary celebrations of World War I, Turkish feminist thinkers have been deeply engaged in

teasing apart the tangled knots of patriarchy, secular republican-
ism, militarism, modernity, ethnicities, religion, and nationalism
in Turkey's still-tumultuous political life. It continues to be a
politically and intellectually risky endeavor.

In addition, reconsidering "Gallipoli" together with its aftermaths alerts us to pay close attention to the ways in which women's
suffrage campaigns were implicated in World War I and can still
be made complicit in sustainable militarism more generally.

It is impossible, I think, to reliably analyze World War I's
multiple wars without taking seriously the dynamics of specific
suffrage campaigns. By the end of World War I, women's right to
cast votes in competitive national elections on the same terms as
men had become an issue for public debate in societies as different
as France, Germany, Ireland, Britain, the United States, Turkey,
Egypt, and China. Already, at the start of the Great War, women
in New Zealand, Australia, and Finland had won the right to vote
on the same terms as men. Four years later, while the ink was not
yet dry on the peace treaty signatures of the all-male delegations
at Versailles, women had gained national voting rights in
Denmark, Moldova, Sweden, Iceland, Russia, Latvia, Lithuania,
Estonia, and Canada. Women in Germany and Austria won their
voting rights a year later. And where women continued to be
barred from casting votes, for instance in France, in Italy, and in
the incompletely decolonized Egypt, the memories of the
sacrifices and contributions that women had made to the war
effort made the bitterness toward men's exclusion of women from
the franchise all the more acute. Trying to accurately remember
diverse, complex suffrage campaigns, and to continue to undertake
rigorous gender/race disaggregation of women's and men's voting
during wartimes and militarized peacetimes, is as relevant to
understanding patriarchy's sustainability and its fragility in the
troubled twenty-first century as it was during World War I.

One might analyze World War I according to its particular moment in international gendered history. One could do the same in analyzing any war. One might ask, for instance, when did the Franco-Prussian War—or the 1960s French Indochina War or the 1990s Yugoslav War or the Syrian War that began in 2011— break out in the ongoing history of relations between women and men, women and the state, women's transnational organizing, and the modernization of patriarchy? By 1914, heated controversies about women's and men's respective political roles were defining public life in most of the countries which became the protagonists in that deadly early-twentieth-century conflict.

The suffrage debates, and the suffrage campaigners and their arch opponents (women and men) who fomented those debates, were central actors in shaping what government elites and diverse ordinary citizens imagined they were going to war to protect. What were men by the thousand dying for, there in the muddy trenches of the Somme? What exactly were the women who served as nurses near the Somme's front lines working so hard to save, when they endured damp, cold, and exhaustion in order to bind the wounds of the men who made it back from the trenches? Furthermore, suffragists themselves were divided over whether shelving their campaigns in the name of wartime national unity was morally necessary or strategically wise—or neither. The divisions among the British suffrage campaigners—most notably between Emmeline and Christabel Pankhurst, on the one hand, and Emmeline's socialist pacifist daughter Sylvia on the other— are perhaps the best documented. But, throughout the years of World War I, women in several countries who were dedicated to women's gaining of the right to vote had to calculate and recalculate the costs and the advantages of calling a wartime moratorium on their suffrage campaigns. Virginia Woolf, for instance, began writing her essays and stories delving into the risks of women's militarization, not, as sometimes supposed, on the eve of World War II, but as early as 1921, in the immediate aftermath of its terrible predecessor.

There is a black and white photograph taken during an extraordinary international women's meeting in The Hague. The year is 1915. Many of the women are looking directly up into the lens of the camera. Some women are seated on the main floor; others fill the balconies above. Some women are hatless; others have kept their hats on for the sake of feminine respectability. One woman up in front sitting on the dais chose to wear an elaborate hat. She was Lucy Thoumaian, representing Armenia; she wore traditional Armenian women's attire to draw attention to the genocidal violence that was that very day being wielded by Ottoman Turks against ethnic Armenians. World War I was at its bloodiest; it took ingenuity, commitment, money, and considerable stamina for these 1,150 women to travel from their own countries to the Netherlands. It also took resilience to withstand the sexist ridicule with which the attendees were taunted. These women were seen by the wagers of war as naïve at best and traitorous at worst. Most of the women who made their ways to The Hague were suffragists, women such as American Jane Addams and Dutch Aletta Jacobs, who had concluded from their years of activism and analysis that masculinized state militarism was a principal obstacle to women's achievement of political equality and, conversely, that the masculinization of political life was a chief cause of militarism.

Outside of Women's Studies, most scholarship on World War I does not give more than a passing mention to the 1915 International Congress of Women at The Hague. Most scholars of that war—and of the wars that have followed it—write and speak as though paying attention to women's transnational wartime analysis and peace activism will reveal nothing about the causes, the crucial dynamics, and the consequences of the war. Yet those same scholars leave their silent presumptions untested. By their inattentiveness, they reinforce the patriarchal notion that war is ungendered, or, if gendered, is affected only slightly by diverse women's idea-driven activism or by the workings of competing masculinities. It has been feminist scholars who have invested the most resources in asking these twin analytical questions: first, under what circumstances, and secondly, in precisely what ways, does the political privileging of certain forms of masculinity—and the denigration of most forms of femininity—make collective violence likely? Posing these twin questions—and pursuing them and widely sharing the findings—not only serves to make wars less inevitable and heroic. It also serves to undermine the perpetuating forces of privileged masculinities.

Finally, there are the gendered aftermaths of World War I: the entrenchment of Japanese colonialism in Korea and Taiwan, the rise of anti-colonial nationalism in Egypt, the consolidation of the secularist Turkish Republic, the institutionalization of Communist Party rule in the expansive multi-ethnic Soviet Union, the stirrings of anti-colonial mobilization in India, Indonesia, and the Caribbean, the invigorating sense among many Americans of their global superiority, the establishment of the new League of Nations (minus the United States), the launch of the promising yet weak Weimar Republic, the simmering of resentment among the war's myriad losers. Thanks to feminist scholarly investigations, we have been learning that every one of these post-World War I developments was shaped by the politics of masculinities and the politics of femininities, and that those politics could be traced back to the gendered dynamics of World War I.

We are also learning that wars do not end for individuals when the cannons are silenced and the treaties are signed. "Veterans"—by which most mean male wartime veterans—become a salient political category. In the 1920s male veterans made government officials nervous, as male veterans still do today. Simultaneously, public caring for mentally and physically wounded soldiers quickly diminished in the post-war era, but demanded feminized attention for years after the war. Men needing care went home not only to Canada, the United States, Britain, Germany, Turkey, Belgium, France, and Russia. They went home to Vietnam, India, then-Rhodesia, South Africa, and scores of other British and French colonies from which imperial armies had recruited troops to fight in Europe. The war might have been declared "over" in the textbooks, but it continued to shape women's relationships to men inside families. Inside families, post-war stories were told and post-war silences were endured. Inside post-war families, wounds were fully accommodated and barely accommodated. Anything that shaped post-World War I women's relationships to each other and to men and boys inside families had an impact on women's relationships to political life.

There is exposing to be done. Who is invited to join the parade? Who is portrayed in the mural, and doing what? Whose struggles and achievements deserve a national holiday? Whose suffering makes it into school textbooks?

Feminists have taught us to ask each of these questions—to pursue and publicize the answers to each. What we can do is make the perpetuation of patriarchal memories and valorizations more clearly the result of particular people's own choices, own wieldings of influence, own dedication of funds. That is a political first step. Then we can call for new memorials, new holidays, new versions of textbooks, new lyrics to national anthems. The recent London sculpture commemorating women munitions workers, the addition of a trio of statues to Boston's Commonwealth Avenue to celebrate three convention-busting women, the deletion of "sons" from the Canadian national anthem—these are just a start.

CHAPTER SIX

A Flick of the Skirt

Marriage continues to be a sticky topic for feminists. Some women's advocates are wary of marriage even in its seemingly progressive guises, while others think that its economic, emotional, and legal benefits should be made available to members of racially and sexually excluded groups.

Despite its patriarchal institutional history, marriage has also been a source of confusion for the most committed of patriarchal policy-makers. On the one hand, marriage has appeared to them to serve as a useful instrument for controlling women's relationships to men, children, property, other women, and the state. On the other hand, patriarchy's sustainers have discovered that marriages, in all their messy lived realities, have often nurtured commitments among both women and men that have subverted loyalty both to a narrowly defined nation, and to the state.

Then there is the added, though usually unspoken, patriarchal worry: what if women-as-wives were to organize politically in order to demand that the nation and the state actually fulfill their promises?

Yet, for all the debates and mobilizations around marriage, the workings of marriage are rarely accorded thoughtful attention by those who comment on "serious" international affairs. It has been left, consequently, to feminist interrogators of marriage—both as an institution and as a site of lived daily experience—to expose the reliance of militarists and militaries, and thus of international policy-makers, on patriarchal marriage. Those feminists who have dug into the gendered dynamics that sustain military bases, foreign deployments, and local military operations have made us more curious about "military wives." They contend that the racially diverse, nationally diverse and class-diverse women in scores of countries who have married soldiers, mostly male soldiers, are worthy of serious inquiry.

To attract our attention, however, these feminists have had to overcome our resistance to being made curious about mere wives. For who, after all, is more subject to international commentators' patriarchal trivialization than a wife?

Not long ago, I attended a meeting in Halifax, Nova Scotia. It was a meeting-after-the-meeting. As the formal academic conference was winding down, a group of local women activists gathered at the university.

Sitting on sofas in a small, comfortable room and fortified by mugs of tea and plates of fruit, seven Halifax women described their years of tracking and publicly challenging militarism in all its Canadian guises as it played out in one of the country's most militarized towns. For 250 years, Halifax's economy has risen and slumped with the cycles of first the British and now the Canadian Navy's shipbuilding programs. Halifax today still hosts several military bases.

Several of these long-time activist women spoke to us of their anti-militarist efforts. Some of the women identified as Anglo-Canadian, others as First Nation Canadian, and still others as

French Canadian. They described their peace vigils in the small park fronting the town's public library.

In recent years, their demonstrations had been protesting then-Prime Minister Stephen Harper's deployments of Canadian forces to support the US-led war in Afghanistan. During the 2006–15 Conservative rule, Canada's military was no longer mandated to prioritize its UN-led international peacekeeping missions. Instead, during this decade, Canadian soldiers' blue helmets were exchanged for olive drab headgear. The Canadian military, according to the Harper government's vision, was to become a "real military": deployed for combat.

This represented far more than a change in federal policy-makers' national security priorities; it amounted to a shift in the Canadian collective national self-image. Prioritizing combat missions over international peacekeeping meant denying a core element of Canada's relationship to the rest of the world, something that distinguished it from its more militarized neighbor to the south. The activists taking part in the Halifax women's peace vigil were part of the resistance to Harper's controversial attempted shift.

These Halifax women's vigil site was on the edge of a busy city street. Along with a steady stream of cars, there was a flow of pedestrians, some of them heading for the public library. As the activists recalled their vigil, they reminded each other of the distinctive reactions of military wives.

Halifax is a small city. Many of the local military bases offer housing for male soldiers' families and, consequently, while these military wives were civilian women dressed in civilian attire, they were personally known to many of the activist women standing vigil. One activist recalled: "I remember when a few of those women from the bases walked by us they would whisper, 'I agree with you, but I can't let anyone know.'" Another activist joined in: "Yes, but I remember that when some of the military wives passed near our vigil they would flick aside the hems of their skirts, as if they were afraid of being tainted by coming in physical contact with us."

This modest Halifax peace vigil became a promising site, I thought, for the attentive feminist investigator. Investigating the militarization of marriages requires paying close attention to each step in the process by which any civilian woman-as-a-soldier's-wife comes to adopt as her own the war-waging interests and perspectives both of her soldier/sailor-husband and her husband's commander. Paying attention—taking seriously—the micro-gestures at this Halifax vigil site also offers a chance to reveal how hard it may be for any country's militarizers to ensure the success of this patriarchal co-opting process. While some women flicked away their skirts from anti-militarist activists, others whispered support.

A flick of a skirt, a whisper of support—these do not readily make their way into most experts' commentaries intended to explain to us how international politics work. These small gestures are all the more difficult to weave into a conventionally coherent political narrative if they each are performed by a civilian woman who has wandered onto the global stage in the role of a wife. Better, imply the conventional experts, to turn our attention back to Canada's shift in national foreign policy priorities.

High theorizing about international politics and noticing the flick of a skirt: potentially, each can enhance our understandings of international politics. The crafting of a theory and the act of noticing a small gesture are both aimed at explaining how and why international relationships operate the way they do, and with what implications. Of course, one cannot simply jump from theorizing to noticing, or vice versa. It takes a lot of theorizing to assign useful meanings to the flick of a skirt, just as it takes repeated acts of careful noticing to build up an explanation to the level of reliable theory, or even of authoritative commentary.

As a political scientist, I was taught that marriage belonged to the sociologists. Political scientists directed their attentions to the public arena. That was the arena whose patterns we were trained to decipher; the fodder for our explanations appeared in that same limited arena. As a corollary, marital relations took place in arenas deemed "domestic" and presumably "private." In this narrow framing, even a peace vigil staffed by local women amidst local women and men going about their local routines scarcely qualified as a "political" space. It took me almost two decades of research, teaching, and listening to realize that this dichotomy between the alleged public sphere and the alleged private sphere hid more about politics than it revealed.

This unrealistically narrow framing of what was worth noticing, what demanded explanation, certainly made it next to impossible to chart the ideas, structures, and dynamics that sustained patriarchy.

Feminists such as Mary Wollstonecraft, Josephine Butler, Elizabeth Cady Stanton, Huda Al Sha'arawi, Virginia Woolf, and Simone de Beauvoir argued—theorized—that the power relationships created and sustained within marriages and inside familial households were essential pillars holding up the patriarchal structures of states, nations, cultural institutions, economies, and international systems; and, they contended, a lot of the beneficiaries of those patriarchal structures knew it.[1] The perceptions of each of these theorists, we now have come (been pushed) to acknowledge, were hindered by the blinders of imperialism, classism, and racism. Yet, for their readers and listeners during their own eras, their insights broke down patriarchal walls and pried open jammed patriarchal doors that had sustained the dual political fiction that marriage was not about power, and that states didn't rely for their own preservation on men's control of marriages.

Evidence supporting these thinkers' political analyses took several forms, one of the most persuasive being the extraordinary efforts the beneficiaries of patriarchy have invested in organizing very particular sorts of relationships between all sorts of racially, economically and ethnically diverse women and similarly diverse men: women as mothers, daughters, wives, mothers-in-law, prostitutes, mistresses, paid and unpaid workers, and domestic servants; men as fathers, sons, husbands, brothel-owners, brothel customers, adulterers, police officers, generals, rank-and-file soldiers, property-owners, paid workers, lawmakers, and judges.

Patriarchy has continued to depend on creating and sustaining an elaborately designed gendered cat's-cradle among these gendered actors. The strings forming this web of relationships can become frayed. They need constant reinforcing. While inattentive, non-feminist political scientists were monitoring elections, reading the fine print in trade agreements, and eavesdropping on war-room debates, these patriarchal actors were devising new self-serving racialized and classed formulas for controlling marriage, divorce, reproduction, child custody, sexuality, and inheritance.

It was feminist observers who prompted me to pull back the curtain on the domestic sphere so that I could see the workings of power inside marriages as *more* than personal interactions, *more* than the stuff of folk tales, novels, gossip, and scandals. These were the thinkers who enabled me to see, there in the myriad domesticated spaces—in the kitchen, in the bedroom, on the household garden plot, in the brothel—the busy hands of state officials, nationalists, captains of industry, military commanders, revolutionary strategists, and electoral campaigners. Suddenly the kitchen, bedroom, brothel, and garden plot looked very political—and crowded.

Most of these early feminist thinkers' works never make their way into international sociology or international politics course syllabi. That, I think, is a loss. Instead, these works are read by members of informal women's book groups and by those undergraduate and postgraduate students, a majority of them women, who enroll in intersectionally framed women's and gender studies courses. Yet these writers' works are informed by, and do shed light on, international affairs. Each of these writers was conscious of the international context within which she was tracking the workings of marriage. Each writer was developing her thoughts about the ways in which the marriage system is designed to sustain patriarchy. Each woman concluded that the power dynamics she was exposing played a crucial role in determining the shape of international affairs.

British thinker Mary Wollstonecraft, for instance, was motivated to write *A Vindication of the Rights of Woman*,[2] her 1792 dissection of the domestic and societal workings of women's political marginalization and forced dependency, by her witnessing of the French revolution and wondering about the gendered assumptions undergirding some of its most prominent male political philosophers. Wollstonecraft was as internationally conscious in her era as any current Egyptian, Syrian, or Tunisian feminist thinker dissecting the gendered dynamics of the Arab Spring uprisings and their suppressions is in our own.

Six decades after Wollstonecraft, British social reformer Josephine Butler dared to compare the political status of women in "respectable" marriages to the status of women in prostitution. Butler (who in 2016 got her own Royal Mail commemorative stamp) sought to mobilize British white middle-class married women in support of their working-class white countrywomen.

She did so as leader of the Anti-Contagious Diseases Acts campaign. Activists inspired by Butler were intent upon overturning the all-male parliament's post-Crimean War's Contagious Diseases Acts, laws which targeted poor women whom local authorities suspected of being prostitutes. Male supporters of the Contagious Diseases Acts claimed that these poor women's sexual practices endangered the health of British military men and thus the security of the empire. After twenty years of campaigning, Butler's Anti-Contagious Diseases Acts campaign won; the still all-male parliament overturned the acts, at least as applied to England.[3] This was international politics.

Also writing in the late nineteenth century, American women's suffrage theorist Elizabeth Cady Stanton delved into the unequal legal and economic relationships within state-sanctioned marriage, chiefly among the country's white women and men. She became convinced that familial patriarchy was a bulwark against women's gaining equality with men in civic life. She waged campaigns for married women's rights to property and married women's rights to divorce. She theorized that patriarchy did not rest simply on the denial of women's suffrage; patriarchy rested equally, she found, on the denial of women's rights as wives. Election rules and divorce laws were best understood as politically mutually dependent.

As a strategist (in partnership with Susan B. Anthony), Stanton was conscious of the international alliances being built among suffrage thinkers and activists who were tracking the causal linkages between inequality within households and inequality within diverse state systems. Anthony thus spoke out against American imperialist intervention in the Philippines during the 1890s. Earlier, Stanton herself was galvanized to work for women's political rights by taking part in one of history's first international social movement gatherings. She crossed the Atlantic to witness at first hand the marginalization of women by the men allegedly committed to social justice who organized the 1840 World Anti-Slavery Convention in London.[4] The transatlantic slave trade, systems of enslaved labor, racial ideologies, the laws governing prostitution, the institution and practices of marriage—increasingly, all five were discussed simultaneously by anti-slavery women activists and thinkers.

Of all these internationally conscious feminist theorists, the most innovative form of expression was crafted by Virginia Woolf. One has to read her *Three Guineas* slowly. Woolf had considered war's effects in the aftermath of the Great War. But it was in the tense 1930s that Woolf was prompted to investigate the deep causes not only of war, but also of militarism. The result is her scathing political critique of the mutually reinforcing causal dynamics between the marginalization of women (she was explicit in her interrogation of white middle-class English society) within families and in the "liberal professions" on the one hand, and, on the other, the masculinized causes of war.

Woolf, a successful novelist, had lived through one world war and by the mid-1930s was growing alarmed at the prospect of another. She was confident that her own intimate male friends would detest *Three Guineas*—precisely because she believed that well-meaning men such as her friends John Maynard Keynes, T.S. Eliot, and Lytton Strachey, and the unthinking women who depended on them, were each willfully oblivious of their own patriarchal complicities in fueling militarization. Woolf was also speaking with urgency to those increasing numbers of middle-class women—"daughters of educated men"—who were on the verge of entering what she described as the "procession" of professional men. She portrayed these men, wearing their bowler hats and carrying their tightly wrapped umbrellas, as they walked briskly to their offices over Waterloo Bridge. The bridge was

Woolf's shorthand for Britain's patriarchal public sphere. Those women about to burst out of their domesticated confines to don robes and uniforms, and thereby to claim authoritative knowledge and a civic voice, were a source of acute worry to Woolf.

Virginia Woolf certainly was not advocating for a return to feminized marital domesticity—far from it. Her investigations threw into sharp relief the patriarchal constraints that such domesticity imposed on women's economic autonomy and, just as importantly, on women's intellectual capabilities. Rather, Woolf was questioning whether the only alternative to patriarchal feminized domesticity was patriarchal masculinized elitism, of a sort that sustained parochial patriotism and legitimized violent militarism. Woolf was writing *Three Guineas* as the storm clouds of war gathered, and just ten years after British women had won the right to vote on the same terms as men. She was warning women against becoming complicit in a system that ultimately despised them. In her distinctive narrative style, Woolf was urging women to assess critically where the bowler-hatted, berobed, and bemedalled masculinized public procession was heading before they too-eagerly joined it:

> On what terms shall we join that procession? Above all, where is it leading us, the procession of educated men?... But, you will object, you have no time to think; you have your battles to fight, your rent to pay, your bazaars to organize. That excuse shall not serve you, madam. As you know from your own experience, and there are facts that prove it, the daughters of educated men have always done their thinking from hand to mouth; not under green lamps at study tables in the cloisters of secluded colleges. They have thought while they stirred the pot, while they rocked the cradle.... Let us never cease from thinking—what is this 'civilisation' in which we find ourselves? What are these ceremonies and why should we take part in them? What are these professions and why should we make money out of them? Where in short is it leading us, the procession of the sons of educated men?[5]

If *Three Guineas* is simultaneously a post-war and pre-war work, Simone de Beauvoir's classic work of political theory, *The Second Sex*, first published in France in 1949, can be read as a post-war work of political theory. Beauvoir's archaeological excavation of the social construction of womanhood was informed by her living through World War II and the Nazi occupation of Paris. Her wartime experiences prompted Beauvoir to explore political power operating in the intimate personal realm and thus to examine women's societal relegation to positions of passivity, weakness, and irresponsibility.

Attentively noticing—taking seriously—the international implications of the apparently trivial minutiae of marital politics, therefore, is not new. Today's explorations are rooted in feminist political theorizing stretching back at least to the 1790s. What is new is the fresh, up-close investigations by feminist researchers into specific militarized marriages. Specifically, these scholars are asking what sort of political power is needed, in specific times and societal settings, to create—and sustain—militarized marriages. They follow up this question with its corollaries: who has what stakes in maintaining each kind of militarized marriage? And: what are the complex, often silent, frequently ambivalent responses of racially, nationally, and class-diverse civilian women to living their lives within such militarized marriages?[26] The investigators have developed an intellectual appetite for "the clumsy banalities" that help constitute international politics.[7]

In most militarized marriages, it is the husband who is playing the most explicitly militarized role—not only as a rank-and-file soldier or uniformed officer, but also as a nuclear weapons scientist, a civilian defense strategist, a defense industry engineer, a defense-budget-promoting legislator, a national security intelligence operator, a private security company contractor, a non-state militia fighter, or a rebel militia fund-raiser. Most of these men are (heterosexually) married, or hope to be. Their manly status—in their own eyes and in the estimation of their colleagues—depends not just on having sexual relations with a woman, but on having a wife, a loyal wife. Her wifely loyalty will become untrustworthy if she does not herself take on the attributes of feminized militarization.

The women who become these disparate militarized men's wives will themselves become militarized to the extent that they willingly absorb their husband's aspirations and values or to the extent that they succumb to the often intense pressures exerted on them to behave as loyally supportive—or at least silent— partners in their husbands' militarized occupations and endeavors. These pressures can extend into widowhood. When a soldier-husband dies in war, his government superiors will expect his new widow to grieve, but not too extravagantly; to express loss, but without trespassing the bounds of patriotism. The British, American, and Russian militaries, among others, have created elaborate organizational procedures and formal ceremonies to keep military widows' (and mothers') expressions of grief suitably expressed and channeled.[8] The uncontrollable, angry military widow inspires fear in the hearts of patriarchal militarizers.

To explore these marital relationships, we need to craft an analytical attentiveness to silences, subtle intimidation, unofficial rewards, seemingly offhand gestures—and to the dismissive flick of a skirt, to the furtively whispered remark.

Feminist ethnographers seem particularly equipped for the job. Perhaps that is because they believe in the power of close observation and give space to descriptive accounts. It is also because they take seriously the political implications of what goes on in domesticated spaces. Take, for example, ethnographers' studies of both US and Russian nuclear weapons facilities and their dependent towns. They reveal in detail the extent to which

Russian and American civilian women as militarized wives have been rewarded, policed, and pressured to play their roles in simultaneously sustaining their husbands' and their governments' militarized missions. Without being propped up by patriarchal marriages, these gender-curious ethnographers show us, these nuclear weapons facilities would not have been able to pursue their states' own militarized objectives.[9]

The most obvious of these diverse militarized marriages are those of civilian women who marry a man in the state's military. These women are commonly—and misleadingly—referred to as "military wives." Misleading, because the phrase denies their actual status as civilian married women. In fact, even a worldly woman, equipped with higher education and her own professional career, can experience culture shock when she goes from being a professional woman respected for her own knowledge and skills to being a military wife. Here is how Rosa Brooks, an American law professor, Defense Department consultant and mother of two daughters, described her own sense of dislocation after she married a man who was a military officer:

> When I married an Army officer, I began to understand, I did more than just acquire new in-laws—I became part of the US Army. I had no enlistment papers and no commission, but I had a rank: "Senior Spouse." ... In some ways, it was like stepping back into the 1950s. On Fort Carson ... being a "spouse" meant, more or less by definition, being a wife.... Husbands did soldier stuff all day, often starting well before first light and coming home exhausted. Officers' wives took care of the kids, hosted "coffees" for other wives, ran Family Readiness Groups, accepted flowers during their husbands' change-of-command ceremonies, and got decorously (or indecorously) plastered at Bunco Nights.[10]

Whereas a few months before her marriage Rosa Brooks had been an expert who was expected to take an active part in debates with senior Defense Department officials over the questionable legality of drone warfare, now, in that same bureaucracy's gendered eyes, she had become a "mere" military wife. In this new world, she discovered, there was little room for distancing oneself from the government's mission. As she soon found, "Fort Carson was an irony-free zone."

Alexandra Hyde obtained permission to live on a British Army base in Germany in the early 2000s in order to study civilian women married to male soldiers in an era marked by the British government's war in Afghanistan. Hyde wanted to explore how these women understood their lives as "military wives."[11]

She discovered that the current British military establishment constantly refined its policies in order to make the army's base "family-friendly." The government's goal was to keep the civilian women attached to their soldier-husbands, despite the stresses produced by having to live away from relatives and friends in the UK, having to defer every day to their husband's command-imposed priorities, and having to take on full responsibility for childcare when their husbands were deployed in Afghanistan.

Hyde also discovered, however, that the women did not think of themselves as mere puppets on the ends of strings pulled by their husbands' commanders and the Ministry of Defence. Most of the women she interviewed told her that they felt as though they had enough autonomy to make meaningful choices, even if the arena for action was constrained by the overlapping expectations of the command, of their often-distracted husbands, and of other wives on the base. These women were also acutely aware of the implications for their own daily lives of their husbands' position in the military's ranking structure: a wife's on-base responsibilities were expected to expand when her husband gained a military rank promotion.

Such mutually reinforcing expectations could prove hard to

resist. Ministry civil servants and her husband's uniformed commanders did not need to apply pressure directly. It was their soldier-husbands and other military wives on the base who imposed rank-defined expectations on wives. The fulfilling of these wifely expectations was assumed to keep the Army's base running smoothly, which was defined as a matter of national security.

Nonetheless, individual women sought some room to exercise their personal preferences. Hyde interviewed a woman she calls Jane whose husband had been promoted to senior officer rank:

> Hyde: Have you avoided becoming a stereotypical [senior soldier's] wife?
>
> Jane: Yes, I've tried to be true to myself, I've done as much as I can, my family are my first priority.... There are a couple of things I haven't done that my predecessors did [laughs], which is go and deliver plants—welcome plants—to new people, and go and knock on their doors. And I tried to do it initially.... I hated it so I stopped doing it.... It wasn't me, so I thought sod it, I don't care!
>
> Hyde: Does [your husband] accept that?
>
> Jane: Yes he does, sometimes I say "oh I don't want to go to coffee morning [with other military wives], I get fed up with it" and he'll say "just keep doing it Jane, just keep showing your face, please, while I'm [in this job]".... There is a rumor that depending on how your wife is and how she behaves depends on how further up the ladder you go. Whether or not there's any truth in that whatsoever I have no idea at all but that's the rumor. [12]

How does one reveal what it took for the British government to join the US-led military operations in Afghanistan? One answer: you pay close attention to who delivers welcome plants to whom. You take seriously which rumors have impacts on whose gendered relationships with whom. And you track the implications of both—for particular women, for particular men, and for militaries in any particular historical circumstances.

Although these British women married to British soldiers had had to give up careers commensurate with their own educations, most of them told Hyde that they felt they had found ways to be useful. Most of the women living on the base, despite not being technically members of the regiment, also seemed to gain emotional satisfaction from being part of the "regimental family." This British regiment (perhaps Scottish) had worked hard for generations to sustain a sense of collective pride and belonging that now extended beyond its male soldiers to their wives. Wollstonecraft, Butler, Stanton, Woolf, and Beauvoir likely would have listened to these British twenty-first-century civilian women with some dismay. These British women had the right to vote on equal terms with their husbands, but there was no evidence of how independent each woman felt when she cast her ballot in Britain's parliamentary elections. These wives of soldiers were not walking across Waterloo Bridge in Woolf's masculinized "procession"; their complicity in militarization did not take the form of donning robes or proudly wearing combat ribbons. Instead, these contemporary women were playing their expected feminized supportive roles as wives, cheering on and caring for their husbands from the sidelines. Still, these women did think; they gave considerable thought to the role of military wife. They weighed its rewards and drawbacks. While there were occasional divorces in the base's families, and while there was a general longing among these women to be back home, there was no rebellion.

Soon after Hyde's stay on the British base, the Ministry of Defence would close down its base in Germany. While the decision was not the product of any military wives' concerted action, the news was greeted by many of the women with relief. Even if the bases were moved back to the UK, however, the militarization of marriages would need to be sustained. It would still require constant official attentiveness and policy action.

British officials in the Ministry of Defence would have to be attentive (though not necessarily responsive) to the wives of men who returned from deployments in Afghanistan (and Iraq, and Northern Ireland) as their ex-soldier husbands struggled to return to civilian life, often with psychological burdens that military planners prefer not to hear about.

Thus it was awkward at best, unnerving at worst, when British military wives went public in 2017 to claim that the British government left them to deal with the often frightening after-effects of their husbands' wartime traumas.[13] "All I did was say, 'Would you like a cup of tea?' and he just grabbed me by the throat and he picked me off the floor and was squeezing my neck with one hand." Nikita Dallison was recalling the terrifying experience of being the object of her traumatized ex-soldier husband's nightmare. Her husband had recently served as a corporal in the British forces in Afghanistan. "I've never seen anyone's eyes like that in my life—he had no idea it was me."

Nikita Dallison had absorbed a lot of worries and done a lot of private caring since her husband returned home. It was what military wives did. It was what their husbands' commanders expected them to do. So long as women as soldiers' and ex-soldiers' wives would internalize the patriarchal belief that wifely care was integral to the marriage contract, and so long as women as militarized wives would adopt the patriarchal values that assigned worth to caring and worrying (and occasionally fearing) in private —so long as both those states of mind could be perpetuated, war-waging governments could underestimate the actual costs of war.

But Nikita Dallison decided to de-privatize her concerns and her anger. She joined a new British women's organization, Combat PTSD Angels. Founded in 2001, by Sue Boardman-McNally, whose soldier husband had served in Northern Ireland, the group's very public demands for increased government attention and resources jeopardized both the patriarchal beliefs and values about good wifely behavior that enabled the British government to undercount the costs of its militarized foreign policies.[14]

The majority of women Alexandra Hyde observed and interviewed when she was living and researching on a British army base in Germany were white and UK-born. But the women married to British soldiers stationed on the base in Germany were not homogeneous. They differed by age, by the numbers and ages of their children, and by the status accorded each civilian woman due to her husband's own military ranks. These women also differed by ethnicity. In addition to the white majority, a small number of Fijian women were living on the base as military wives. Hyde found that most of these Fijian women, who were there because they had married Fijian men serving as soldiers in the British regiment, felt only tangentially part of the regiment's daily social life and carefully honed culture. By the time the British Army went to war in Afghanistan in late 2001, its ranks included growing numbers of men (and a few women) recruited from the Commonwealth. Both British and private security company recruiters admire what they take to be Fijian masculinity. They see ethnic Fijian men as prime enlistees into their militarized forces.

In her studies of the gendered dynamics that sustained Fiji's militarization, the late Teresia Teaiwa noted that Fijian women as military wives today try to weigh which of three current options is better for their families—their husband soldiering for Fiji's military (and perhaps gaining extra pay when he is sent overseas on UN peacekeeping missions), their husband soldiering for the British Army, or their husband soldiering for one of the burgeoning globalized private military companies. The Fijian women married to Fijian male soldiers are practical about marriage. They weigh the advantages and the costs of each militarized option for themselves, their husbands, and their children.[15]

For those non-British women whose husbands have enlisted in the British Army, a chief cost may come in the form of social isolation. Vron Ware, a British researcher, has investigated the lives of Commonwealth men—from Nepal, Fiji, Ghana, Jamaica —who have joined the British Army during the years of the war in Afghanistan, and of their wives, who followed them to Britain.[16] Many of these women discovered that there were constraints they could not have foreseen when they made their initial marital calculations. One Fijian military wife, Kasa, described the culture shock she experienced when she migrated from Fiji to Britain to follow her soldier-husband:

> Here the poor wife takes her children to school and sits at home. Most work in care homes, that's all they can do. They are well above that level. In fact, most wives, their educational background is higher than their husbands'. Most of us gave up good jobs back home—in banks, government, airlines, highly qualified jobs. We are doing nothing here.[17]

Britain's Ministry of Defence, whose officials since the 1990s had calculated that recruiting men from Commonwealth countries was an efficient strategy for filling the Army's ranks, did not invest a great deal of thought in these men's spouses. They imagined, instead, that these women would find their own ways of coping. That neglect was part of the government's national defense efficiency formula. They were caught off-guard when some of these Fijian and Nepalese women began to speak out in public about their disenchantment with their lives as military wives.

State militaries constantly refine their recruiting and basing formulas, at home and abroad. Each configuration requires a distinct form of militarized marriage politics. It is all too easy to imagine that women married to any state's soldiers are chiefly interesting only in so far as they must adjust to, cope with, that state's military strategy. Gender impact analysis is, of course, an important scholarly and political undertaking. Feminist theorizing, however, is about more than consequences, it is about causes. Wollstonecraft, Butler, Stanton, Woolf, and Beauvoir have taught us to track the causal drivers of power systems. They have argued that, to explain how and why power operates the ways it does, we must take seriously the workings of patriarchy. We must invest intellectual energy in investigating how surprisingly flexible power systems, which privilege certain forms of masculinities while subjugating all forms of femininity, are created and then sustained. To do this, they discovered, the straight-line narrative is not sufficient.

Thus, in analyzing over time the politics of marriages in any national—or internationally mobilized and commanded—military, it is not enough simply to explore how women adjust to each new basing strategy. Instead, we need to be curious about how women married to soldiers think about and interact with their society's feminist movements. We need to pay attention to each state military's strategists as they go about designing and redesigning systems that enable their male soldiers (in the early 2000s, no state military has even a quarter of its full-time active duty ranks filled with women soldiers) to fulfill their masculinized desire to marry and yet, simultaneously, control those soldiers' wives so that they do not compromise the military's statist mission. This has become harder to do as more and more of those women have had access to secondary and even university educations, and absorbed ideas about the advantages of having their own paid jobs, of being free to seek a divorce, and of exercising the full range of citizen's rights.

States are not the only authorities running military bases. Currently, the UN Security Council's state members authorize multiple military peacekeeping operations, each calling on member states to contribute contingents of its own soldiers to serve overseas under UN command. Family members do not accompany these UN soldiers. Every UN peacekeeping operation depends on women as military wives accepting lives as *de facto* single mothers at home. In August 2015, according to the UN's "Peacekeeping Fact Sheet", there were sixteen UN peacekeeping missions, operating from the Sinai to South Sudan. Those missions were being carried out by 90,889 uniformed soldiers (as well as 13,550 police officers and 1,806 military observers), a majority of whom were from less economically developed countries. Despite external pressures by women's advocates to integrate more women into the UN's peacekeeping operations, in 2014, according to the UN document "Women in Peacekeeping," of all these UN peacekeeping military personnel, 97 percent were men, while only 3 percent were women. Many of those men on the ground, carrying out the UN Security Council's state members' military mandates, were married. Extra pay earned on overseas missions was intended to be sufficient to support families back home and purchase the cooperation of these soldiers' wives.

We know woefully little about those women and what it has taken to keep them supportive of their blue-helmeted husbands' foreign deployments. The conventional narrative crafted by commentators speaks only of the "Troop-Contributing Countries". It does not have the capacity to look into, much less explain, the causal dynamics that involve peacekeeping male soldiers' relationships with their wives and the efforts of particular governments to influence those relationships so they can deploy their troops on peacekeeping missions. As more reports have surfaced of male peacekeeping soldiers' engagement in sexual abuses while deployed abroad, it is likely that those marital dynamics have become more, not less, complicated. The skills required for reliable international political analysis will have to become all the more sophisticated.

In this same era of international militarized politics, several major military powers have been altering their domestic and overseas basing and deployment strategies. In the name of anti-terrorism, French military planners have expanded their military's operations in French-speaking Africa, their largest base being in Mali. The British government has been shrinking its overseas military bases, though not its militarized foreign policy. The Chinese government's national security officials are building new military facilities on coral reefs in the South China Sea, while also seeking military access to facilities in the South Pacific. Under Vladimir Putin, the Russian military has secured its expansive naval base in Sevastopol by forcibly annexing the Crimea. Simultaneously, it has re-activated its naval base at the port of Tartus on the western coast of Syria. Each of those French, Chinese, and Russian military bases can be adequately understood only if their racialized, gendered, interlocking politics of marriage and prostitution are investigated.

The US government, whose military has the world's most globalized network of bases, has been negotiating new basing agreements with multiple governments at the same time as it has been designing new sorts of military bases. Thus, as basing scholar David Vine has revealed, in 2015 the US Defense Department operated full-fledged military bases in Turkey, Okinawa, South Korea, Djibouti, Diego Garcia, South Korea, Colombia, Bahrain, Honduras, Australia, Iraq, and Guam. At the same time, the Defense Department has created scores of infrastructurally more modest and socially less visible "lily pad" or "light footprint" military bases—in Kenya, Burundi, Uganda, Liberia, Aruba, and Jordan.[18] Family housing and services are being shrunk by the Defense Department designers, or disposed of altogether, on all these bases. The effect is an intensification of the masculinized militarized climate on each base and, necessarily, the escalation of state demands on those women married to the deployed and contracted men and left behind to accept longer stretches of single motherhood at home.

In the Gulf state of Djibouti alone, in 2016, there were Spanish, French, and US military bases. The Saudis and the Chinese are soon to arrive. Chinese defense officials are currently building their first overseas military base in the Gulf state of Djibouti, and this will become the close neighbor of the US military base in Djibouti, Camp Lemonnier.[19] Most of these Djibouti bases are, or soon will be, staffed overwhelmingly by men. Each of these governments' overseas bases is markedly masculinized, several combining masculinized troops with masculinized contractors. It is not clear what proportion of these uniformed and civilian militarized men working in Djibouti are married. Their wives, however, have been left at home. Dutch feminist journalists have documented widespread prostitution, dependent on the exploitation of refugee Somali and Sudanese girls and women stranded in Djibouti.[20] Prostitution, marriage, and militaries—feminists have learned to always investigate the relationships of each to the other in making visible the actual workings of international politics.

As David Vine explains, these current Russian, French, British, American, Saudi, and Chinese overseas military basing formulae rely upon the patriarchal assumption that most deployed male soldiers are able to leave wives and children thousands of miles behind for weeks and months without being distracted by divorce filings.[21] To say that any state relies on patriarchal relationships to fashion and implement its national security doctrine is to talk about multi-stranded causations, not merely impacts. If enough women-as-wives begin to resist, entire foreign policy strategies could be up-ended.

Since militarizers' attempts to control women in marriages—and women's responses to those efforts—are crucial to conducting both domestic and overseas military operations, anyone who claims to offer an authoritative commentary on those operations needs to exercise curiosity about the politics of perpetuating marriage itself.

Marriage was, and still is, characterized by feminists from scores of cultures as the site of states' control over women's lives. Marriage also, feminists have revealed, has bestowed on many men material, sexual, and political special privileges and, by so doing, helped sustain women's oppression, impoverishment, and isolating domestication. Furthermore, marriage has been criticized by feminists for serving as whole societies' validation for presumptions about the inferiority of anything that can be domesticated or feminized. On the other hand, by becoming a feminized married adult—a "wife"—a woman might gain at least some of the benefits offered to women by their patriarchal societies: social respectability, masculinized protection, legalized motherhood, and second-hand economic security. In practice, these benefits may turn out to be precarious, and they may be bought at a substantial personal cost to a woman. But they are not inconsequential. When certified with a religious seal of approval and soft-lit by a romantic narrative, the benefits of marriage for women can appear attractive indeed.

It is no wonder, then, that many parents worry when their daughters reach marital age without being married. It is common for women to pity a woman who "has not found a husband," although such pity can be tinged with suspicion if that unmarried woman is perceived as a rival for their own husbands' affections.

Marriage—the benefits flowing from it, the aspirations for it, the precariousness of it—has provided fuel for divisions between women themselves. Patriarchy's sustainability relies on many women being suspicious of other women, seeing other women as their rivals for men's affections. The storylines of folk tales, operas, novels, movies, and television serials are rife with these feminized suspicions and rivalries.

Given marriage's real-life benefits, it is not surprising that the "right to marry" has been a goal for both anti-racism movements and gay rights activists. Challenging anti-miscegenist and homophobic laws has proved a galvanizing cause. In the mid-twentieth century, many women joined with male allies to overturn their governments' laws prohibiting marriages between people of different races. Likewise, in the early decades of the twenty-first century many straight feminists joined LGBT activists to energize "marriage equality" campaigns.

It is marriage's apparent double-edged sword that has prompted some feminists, nonetheless, to hoist warning flags over the gay marriage movement, urging their gay, lesbian, and transgender allies to pause, to consider whether the institution of state-regulated marriage really should be accorded such political primacy.[22] Legalized gay marriages have enabled thousands of LGBT people for the first time to gain access to pensions, inheritance, child custody, hospital visiting privileges, tax breaks, and health care not available to unmarried women and men in their countries. Expanded access to state-recognized marriage also has enabled lesbians, gay men and transgender people to openly express love and affection for their partners. Once marriage between same-sex partners has been legalized, even some outspoken feminist critics of marriage have married, not so that they could openly express their commitment to each other, but precisely because it is only as a married couple in the eyes of the state that they could be assured of having access to these material benefits and protections.

Unquestioned enthusiasm for a state-certified coupling system—marriage—nevertheless does risk undermining feminists' efforts to break open the narrow concept of the "family," to make families more porous and inclusive. Furthermore, the new validation of state-regulated marriage between same-sex couples can further marginalize those individuals who are making their lives outside of marriage.

It may seem unfair to place militarized marriages at the center of this wider discussion of marriage politics. Militaries, after all, have the capacity to exert exceptional control over not only their soldiers, but also the women and men who marry them. Yet militaries have not created state-regulated marriage. They have not set the basic ground rules of legally recognized marriage. *Militaries use the legal and cultural materials at hand.* Taking seriously the complex lives and daily calculations of diverse women married to a wide range of militarized men and women should enable us to ask sharper questions about all marriages and about state-regulated marriage in all its modern forms.

Feminists who are working hard in so many countries to destabilize patriarchy urge us all to keep asking this crucial question: under what conditions is state-regulated marriage less a site of genuine liberation, and more a site for updated patriarchy? This question can prove awkward to ask. It constitutes a political act to ask it—and to grapple with the answers.

CHAPTER SEVEN

A Winding Road to Feminist Consciousness

Self-reflection can be indulgent. It can place one at the center of the universe. Always a bad move. Yet reflecting on one's own winding journey can be discomfiting. It can make one freshly curious about why one was so unquestioning or inattentive for so long.

Now we're getting somewhere.

"What kind of name is 'Enloe'?" my college classmates asked in a chorus. They had been given an assignment to track down the national or ethnic origins of the family names of every member of the freshman class. I remained the lone puzzle. I passed along the family lore. Enloe, my father had told us, was a Scots Irish name. My classmates looked at me skeptically. Who had ever heard of an "Enloe" among the haggis, heather, and peat?

The Enloes (in reality, a mixture of Scots Irish, English, and Dutch) seemed to have been a restless lot. They sailed to the New World in the 1630s. By the 1840s, many of their descendants had become farmers in Missouri and Kentucky, on what Euro-Americans deemed "the frontier." There is even a tale told of young Nancy Hanks working as a laborer on the farm owned by an Abraham Enloe. It was he, so the story goes, who became the biological father of Abraham Lincoln. A number of social media amateur historians have embraced this story.

While the Enloe family history remains fuzzy, the narrative helped me understand my father. And that, of course, is one of the functions of family history. It seemed to explain my own father's restlessness, his striving to move from the periphery to the established center, though he often managed to subvert his own efforts. He was an American, impoverished by the Depression, who earned his medical degree in Germany. He was a Midwesterner, who chose to make his way in New York. He was a soldier in the US Army in World War II, but joined the "Chindits," an irregular behind-enemy-lines air commando unit in Burma, made famous by Milt Caniff's cartoon strip *Terry and the Pirates* (my father was "Doc"). His proudest moment was representing the American Chindits in the London funeral parade for Lord Mountbatten.

It was my father and his family who seemed to have been engaged with history. Only belatedly, in the early 1980s, as I started to write what became my first feminist-informed book, *Does Khaki Become You?*, did I start to see my mother in history. But to do that I had to push my father's story into the wings; I had to find a way to make my mother's story worthy of occupying center stage.[1] I started by rereading my mother's diary entries for the years of World War II, to assign the American feminized "home front" added narrative and analytical weight.

My mother was a native Californian, born in 1907 in Altadena, in the foothills of Los Angeles. She spent most of her childhood just up the coast in Santa Barbara, where her father had bought a hotel, The Upham. My mother's father was a Goodridge, whose ancestors left Bury St. Edmunds during the English agricultural recession of the 1630s. By the 1860s, their descendant, young Ira Colby Goodridge, my mother's father, was a teenage boy soldier in an upstate New York Union Army regiment. It appears he never was deployed to a battlefield. My mother's side of the family has not had war stories to pass down through the generations.

After his first wife died, Ira joined the 1890s migration to California, hoping to make a new life. There, Ira, the widower, met and married Frances, the daughter of Welsh immigrants and a divorcee, who also had migrated westward (from Minnesota) in search of a new beginning. In 1898, before migrating to California, Frances had travelled to Europe, in the company of a young woman friend and her mother. They had visited the grave sites of famous British writers whom they had read, Robert Burns and Robert Louis Stevenson. I only came across Frances's account of this European trip a decade after my mother's own death, when it turned up among my father's medical books.

Ira and Frances had a daughter, my mother, Harriett. By the time young Harriett was twelve she had lost her mother to cancer and her father had become a double widower. Ira invited a young Navy widow from New England, Lil Holden, to come out to California to work at The Upham and act as a surrogate mother to young Harriett. Lil Holden is the person, I think, who gave my mother her sense of adventure: with Lil, teenage Harriett rode horseback on the Santa Barbara beaches; it was Lil who approved of her teenage charge driving her car "Betsy" up the coast to enter the all-women's Mills College; it was with Lil that my mother travelled by ocean liner to Europe in the early 1930s; and it was Lil who encouraged my mother to enroll in a Harvard-affiliated early childhood education graduate program, a program which included doing volunteer work at the Ruggles Street Settlement House. Later, my mother got a Depression-era teaching job at one of the early Montessori schools back in California.

On a second European trip Harriett met a lively American medical school student outside a Heidelberg restaurant. Cortez

Enloe and Harriett Goodridge married after just six months of courtship and then lived for three years in Germany, tracking with alarm the rise of Hitler.

My mother was not one to dramatize her life. By the time I was growing up in Manhasset in the 1940s and '50s, she had become a Long Island suburban housewife, driving cancer patients to radiation appointments, later delivering Meals on Wheels and chauffeuring our girls hockey team to games in her Ford station wagon. Only occasionally would she tell funny tales about driving "Betsy" up and down the California coast, or getting caught out during a Mills fire drill, or being stuck for hours in a Paris elevator. Of course, it was only when I belatedly gained a feminist consciousness that I could look back and see that the conventional narrative of the American nuclear family is more myth than fact. This growing understanding motivated me to make visible my mother's experiences in many of my own writings (most recently, in the short piece on the militarization of civilian tourism that forms Chapter Four of this book).

Taking my mother's experiences seriously led to my exploring the militarization of marriages. It made me alert to what feminist historians have been telling us now for four decades: pay attention to the feminized silences—not just silences due to oppression, but silences flowing from many women's belief that their wartime experiences don't "matter"—that they are merely private, trivial, apolitical. Men wage wars; women simply "cope" with wartime. Coping does not make for exciting history.

Still, I have tried to be fair to my father's legacy. For instance, it was his telling of his experiences in World War II Burma that, even as a ten-year-old, awakened my interest in the Gurkhas. Their bravery and stalwart loyalty have made these British-enlisted Nepalese male soldiers iconic. I didn't see my first Gurkhas until seventeen years later when I was in Kuala Lumpur, doing my dissertation research. A group of Gurkha soldiers were drilling on the central *padang* under the tropical sun. An expatriate British white woman standing next to me exclaimed admiringly, "They are brave, aren't they, marching in this heat dressed in wool uniforms?" Taking Gurkhas seriously has prompted me to explore the intertwined histories of colonialism, post-colonialism, militarized racism, and militarized masculinities.[2] Since becoming a feminist, I have tried to make visible the British military's dependence on Nepalese women as Gurkha wives.[3]

Manhasset, Long Island, was a quintessential post-World War II suburban town. We were taught no local history in our public schools. As children, we all thought Manhasset had been an Indian chief. Manhasset High School's sports teams were named the "Indians." Actually, Manhasset means "island neighborhood" in the Matinecock language. Betty Friedan would have recognized the gendered dynamics that underpinned life in Manhasset. *The Feminine Mystique* described the limitations experienced by white middle-class women living in similar Westchester suburbs, just across Long Island Sound.[4] My mother and many of her suburban friends were college graduates. They poured their skills into unpaid local volunteer work. They also took the Long Island Rail Road into New York for theater and concerts. None of them, however, took the morning commuter train into the city. That was the masculinized transit, carrying their husbands into the city for their office jobs. My mother and her women friends drove their husbands down to the station on weekday mornings and then waited for the outbound, feminized train which would bring the African American women from Queens to clean Manhasset's middle-class homes.

My mother would have been at the station to pick up Betty Scudder. My younger brother and I learned to call her "Betty." She called my mother "Mrs. Enloe." William Levitt, the suburban developer, had bought former estate land in Manhasset from the railroad barons, the Vanderbilts, to build 1940s upscale suburban homes for the young families then moving out on the island from New York, Jackson Heights, and Brooklyn. He gave all the streets of his development English names. We lived on Aldershot Lane; nearby were Essex, Sussex, and Chapel. Levitt included a "maid's room" in his suburban home design. It was a room off the kitchen, with its own bath. Betty Scudder didn't stay overnight, but this was the room in which she changed her clothes every Monday, Wednesday, and Friday. Years later, when I began to delve into the lives and politics of women from the Philippines, Sri Lanka and Mexico migrating to work as domestic workers, I thought again of Betty Scudder.

As late as the 1960s, Manhasset was a racially segregated New York suburb. The small Black community was confined to a neighborhood called Spinney Hill. There were no African American families in our neighborhood, nor did we have any Black classmates in our elementary school. Only in junior high and high school were Manhasset's public schools racially integrated. Until then, I was not conscious of local racialized segregation. The differences I was aware of were between Catholics, Protestants, and Jews. My best neighborhood pals, Richie and Alfie Ross, were Catholics; they went to St. Mary's, the town's parochial school. Manhasset of the 1940s and '50s was also marked by anti-Semitism. There were three boating clubs nearby. Two of them, the Manhasset Bay Yacht Club (to which my parents belonged) and the Port Washington Yacht Club, were white and Christian. The third, the Knickerbocker Yacht Club, was white and Jewish. By the 1950s, when I was in high school, there were several Jewish families in our neighborhood, but the fact that they were Jewish was always mentioned. Christmas pageants remained an annual feature of our public elementary school calendar.

My parents were avid newspaper and magazine readers. Copies of the *New York Times* and the *New York Herald Tribune* arrived on our doorstep every morning. I caught the newspaper bug. Friends today joke about my habitual underlining and clipping of the *Times*. I have favorite journalists, including Sabrina Tavernise, Carlotta Gall, and Alissa Rubin. I read the fruits of investigative reporting slowly. I want to know how certain unspoken assumptions become a collective "common sense." I want to know who has made what fateful (usually imagined to be "minor") decisions. So I read long *Times* articles in which careful journalists (overseen by careful editors) track the militarized arming of American local police departments, or the creation of exploitative workplaces which place at risk Bangladeshi garment factory employees or Korean American nail salon workers.[5]

Decisions. Exposing decisions and decision-makers is, I think, a feminist commitment. It reveals that the racism, class inequality, and, of course, sexism that commonly pass as "tradition," "nature," and "culture" can be traced back to deliberate actions by specific individuals who are seeking to protect their own interests or the interests of the institutions they serve. Holding accountable all sorts of decision-makers for their choices—including their choosing neglect, denial, and inaction—is crucial, I've come to believe, for sustaining civic trust.

When I entered Connecticut College in 1956, Vassar was still an all-women's college. Douglass, Pembroke, and Radcliffe still were autonomous all-women's colleges within their larger masculinized universities. I chose to go to Connecticut in part, I think, because I had heard my mother's stories about her years at Mills. I also imagined that the social pressures so prevalent at a co-ed public high school would be fewer at an all-women's college.

Although it was then a proudly women's college and many of its professors were among the first American women to earn PhDs in their fields, Conn's students in the late '50s were taught no women's history and assigned scarcely any women authors. We didn't read Mary Wollstonecraft in Miss Dilley's political theory course, nor Virginia Woolf in Miss Noyes' English courses, nor did we explore the US, British, or French women's suffrage movements in Miss Holborn's comparative politics course. Was it perhaps that these women, who certainly treated us, their women students, seriously, nonetheless had achieved their then-exceptional academic status by not taking seriously women as intellectual *subjects?*

What these remarkable women faculty members did do, however, was invite prominent women to campus as speakers: Alice Paul, Eleanor Roosevelt, and Hannah Arendt. Two of these three are now due to appear on the redesigned US currency. It is thoroughly embarrassing today to admit that neither Paul's nor Roosevelt's visits made any lasting impression on youthful callow me. Alice Paul's name was totally unfamiliar. I had never heard of the Pankhursts, forced feeding, or the Women's Party. It wasn't until twenty years later, when feminist historians woke me up to the transnational histories of multiple suffrage movements, that I began assigning books to my own students on the Egyptian, Brazilian, and British suffrage movements, doing a belated penance for my undergraduate ignorance. I did know of Roosevelt, but only as a cartoonish figure of ridicule, not as a feminist, social reformer, or a major contributor to the United Nations. Only decades later, reading Blanche Weisen Cook's engrossing biography, did I realize why Connecticut College's women faculty would have been so excited to have ER on campus.[6]

Hannah Arendt came to campus in the depths of the Cold War, only several years after she had published *The Origins of Totalitarianism.*[7] I had a hard time following her talk because her ideas were far beyond my intellectual capacities. I strained to understand. I took notes furiously. It was altogether thrilling.

Several years later, taking Sheldon Wolin's political theory courses at Berkeley, I had the chance to read Arendt's books. This was also a time—in the mid-1960s—when Arendt was writing essays regularly for the *New Yorker* and the *New York Review of Books*. I took those issues to Berkeley coffee houses to read and underline. I still have a now-yellowing file of all Arendt's magazine essays.

I loved college—the studying, friendships, singing groups, student government, and sports teams. All of it. In the summer between my junior and senior years, I had a Washington internship at the Department of Agriculture, a mind-expanding experience for a suburbanite who could barely distinguish between azaleas and lilacs. I became a gofer for a group of male agriculture specialists from Ghana, Turkey, and Indonesia, countries about which I knew nothing. In the late 1950s, Washington was still a racially segregated city. Civil servants warned me not to go out for meals with any of the visiting agriculturalists, since restaurants were sure to deny seating to a young white woman in the company of men of color. The Indonesian member of the group, Gelar Wiratmaja, was a fisheries specialist. He befriended me that summer. He was dismayed that I hadn't heard of the Indonesian revolution against the colonizing Dutch, but endeavored to tutor me in Indonesian politics. His efforts had a lasting impact.

I became a political scientist when I entered the University of California, Berkeley, in 1961. Thanks to the spark lit by Gelar Wiratmaja, I combined political science with Asian studies. This combination meant that I had to study histories, cultures, identities, literatures, and political economies. "Politics" could never realistically be shrunken down to elections, armed conflicts, state security, and public policies. Thus when I was doing my dissertation research in Malaysia—on the ethnic politics of education, an intensely fraught issue—I had to understand the political economies of rubber and tin, the legacies of British colonialism, and the complex workings of ethnic identities. I did not, however, interview a single Malaysian woman.

A broad understanding of what one must explore in order to get one's arms around political life stood me in good stead when I later encountered feminism, for one of the most profound—and discomfiting—feminist insights has been that the conventional (patriarchal) definition of "politics" is unrealistically narrow. Worse, this conventional patriarchal imagining of what constitutes the study of political life serves to hide power—myriad forms of power. Feminists seek to investigate—and expose—the workings of power, all kinds of power.

But I'm jumping ahead. There was no talk of feminist insights at Berkeley in the early 1960s. Of the fifty tenure-track faculty members in the political science department, not one was a woman and not one introduced gender analysis into his studies of politics. And, to my shame, I did not notice. That is one of the ways patriarchal institutions sustain themselves—by making lives lived inside them so exciting, challenging, and occasionally rewarding (Sarah Schumer and I were the first women grad students to be selected by the faculty to be head teaching assistants in political science) that one scarcely notices the deep-seated workings of masculinization.

Two things happened during my Berkeley years that pushed me to realize that academic work called for the taking of political responsibility. First was the sudden eruption in 1965 of what came to be known as the Free Speech Movement. At noontime I was staffing a modest bridge table (distributing flyers for a new off-campus play-reading group) on the edge of campus when a biology grad student named Mario Savio, staffing a nearby table, resisted the dean's demand that we disband. His refusal sparked a campus-wide fierce debate about the meanings of higher education, the rights of free speech, and eventually, the roles of city police on campuses. I joined the student strike. The political science faculty was deeply split over the Free Speech Movement.

I kept my distance, however, from the social life within Berkeley's Free Speech Movement. I didn't have the words for it then, but I had a feeling it was sexualized and masculinized. Only later, reading feminist studies of nationalist, civil rights, and labor movements around the world, did I have the concepts to make sense of that intuitive distancing.

The escalating war in Vietnam was the second occurrence during those Berkeley years that made me aware of the political responsibility accompanying an academic career. The US government was actively courting Southeast Asian specialists. I knew I had to take a stand: was the armed conflict in Vietnam an expression of continuing post-colonial nationalism? Alternatively, was it merely one more "domino" falling in the wake of the Communist Party's victory in China? Nationalism and revolution—these were topics of heated scholarly debate with profound political implications. Chalmers Johnson, a Japan and China specialist, was among my principal mentors. At the time, there were so few scholars of Vietnam writing in English that we all tried to apply lessons we had drawn from studying upheavals in China, the Philippines, and Indonesia. Again, however, it was only later that I realized that none of us was curious about women participants in, or the gendered ideologies propelling, either revolutions or nationalist movements. When I later offered my first courses in the comparative politics of women, I tried to compensate for this early lack of curiosity by assigning new feminist histories of the French, Russian, and Chinese revolutions, revealing women's revolutionary thinking, women's contributions, and women's repeated post-revolution disappointments.

Thus I began my academic researching and teaching career as a comparative politics specialist, focusing on Asia and ethnic politics. This was at a time when dozens of countries were throwing off colonial rule and undertaking the challenging processes of building viable nation-states and rolling back myriad forms of poverty. My initial faculty post was at Miami University of Ohio, where the fifteen men in the department had never had a woman colleague before but were very welcoming. At Miami, besides my courses on Asian politics, I had the chance to introduce a new university course in Black politics. The Black officials and movement leaders from Dayton and Cincinnati whom I invited to speak in the course were—yes, you guessed it—all men. Later, when Black feminists such as Barbara Smith, Beverly Smith, and Kate Rushin opened my eyes to the long and continuing political theorizing and organizing done by African American women, I thought back on my choices there in Ohio and realized how easy it was, in the pursuit of alleged educational innovation, to perpetuate patriarchal presumptions about who was "interesting."[8]

During a Fulbright, I taught at the University of Guyana, on the far edge of the Caribbean. The students were Afro-Guyanese and Indo-Guyanese male civil servants. They were not comfortable with each other. The course was held at night in a classroom next to a large Booker sugar plantation. During that year I learned about the ethnic politics of both sugar and bauxite, while being tutored in the mysteries of cricket by the two young children of my Indo-Guyanese landlord. On Sunday afternoons, we three would gather around the radio to listen to the BBC's coverage of the West Indian cricket team's matches.

While still in Guyana I accepted a faculty post at Clark University, near Boston. By this time, I was lucky enough to have published several books, all cross-national in scope, each exploring the workings of racism and ethnocentrism, yet each devoid of any gender analysis, thereby making women invisible. In these pre-feminist books I also made men-as-men invisible. Men were simply peasants or landlords or insurgents or party leaders. When I finally applied a feminist curiosity to my teaching and research, nonetheless, I kept ethnicity and race on my mind. All the years of delving into the complexities of identities, discriminations, and elite-devised divisions of labor helped inoculate me against treating "women" as homogeneous or as forming an inevitable sisterhood. A sense of solidarity among diverse women, I've learned, has to be created—and then recreated.

During my initial year at Clark, I subscribed to the debut issues of both *Ms.* magazine and Billie Jean King's *Women's Sport.* A nascent feminist consciousness was finally beginning to bubble up. But it was undergraduate women students who pushed it to the surface. Hearing that there was something called "women's studies" being launched at nearby University of Massachusetts, a dozen undergrad women in 1974 persuaded a dean to get a handful of us women faculty members together for a bag lunch. The students were persuasive. Three of us agreed to create Clark's initial courses in what would become the university's lively women's studies program: Women in American Politics, Fiction by Women Writers, and my own Comparative Politics of Women.

Our excitement was contagious. Soon other faculty members were launching their own women's studies courses. At least as important, we created a lively—though unfunded—women's studies faculty group, which reached out to interested faculty at Worcester's other six colleges. I joined the fledgling National Women's Studies Association and subscribed to US and British feminist journals, such as *Sojourner, Spare Rib,* and *Trouble and Strife.* I soon became a regular at New Words, the famous Cambridge feminist bookstore. When I was in London, generous British feminist scholars and activists took me under their wings, making sure I engaged with their intense debates over lesbianism and heterosexism, radical feminism, and socialist feminism.

I avidly read and listened to Bea Campbell, Dale Spender, and
Sally Alexander.

But my publishing was out of sync with my expanded curiosity.
When Penguin sent me the page proofs for *Ethnic Soldiers* (1980) so
that I could do my own indexing, I frantically tried to find, in the
hundreds of pages dissecting racisms and ethnic hierarchies in
diverse militaries, some mention of women. With my new
feminist consciousness, I didn't want the "W"s confined to
"Walloons," "World War I," and "World War II." With a sigh of
feminist relief, I found I had (unwittingly) mentioned "women" in
the chapters on the Gurkhas and on the white racist military of
then-Rhodesia.

Women's studies' theorizing and women activists' thinking
have fed each other in virtually every country. The movement
made its biggest impact on my own women's studies academic
involvement when my Chilean anthropologist Clark colleague,
Ximena Bunster, came into my office one afternoon, closed the
door, and began to describe the sexually intimidating behavior of
her male department chair. Ximena was an exile, driven out of
Chile by Pinochet. This meant that her position at a US university
depended on a visa, a visa that would disappear if a department
chair decided to end her visiting professor's contract.

It was 1979. Neither Ximena nor I had any concept to explain
what she was experiencing. Thanks to my friends at New Words
Bookstore, Ximena and I were introduced to a few Boston
feminists who had formed a group to support local women factory
workers coping with sexualized abuse by their male foremen.
They called themselves AASC, Alliance Against Sexual
Coercion. They asked Ximena to describe what she was
experiencing in her university workplace. After listening carefully, they told us, "That is sexual harassment." We had never
before heard those two words put together.

For the next four years, inside and outside academia, we had to grapple with this unfamiliar form of power abuse, one that did not fall neatly on any left-right or hawk-dove spectrum. What was the difference between flirting and harassment? Was sexual harassment more about power than sex? Could a prominent leftist professor be an abuser? Were university administrators (and trustees and their lawyers) who treated a woman's charges of sexual harassment dismissively themselves guilty of sexual harassment? If these questions sound familiar today, in 2017, it is because we all are still trying to understand how patriarchal power works and the masks the wielders of it don to escape accountability.

That grappling during the early 1980s divided households, academic associations, campuses, and peace organizations. It was exhausting and exhilarating. Ximena survived the prolonged, bitter ordeal and returned to Santiago to become active in the Chilean women's movement that was so central to bringing down the junta. The full story of the Clark sexual harassment case— posters, articles, court briefs, donation ledgers—is now in the collections of Harvard's Schlesinger Library of American Women's History, available for all researchers to mine.

I learned during these years how crucial the fashioning of concepts can be: they make the invisible visible and, in so doing, enable people to move beyond either denial or self-blame, toward collective action and meaningful change. "Date rape," "glass ceiling," "domestic violence," "double day," "feminization of poverty," "mansplaining," "systematic wartime rape"—I'm continuing to learn not only the value of accurate conceptualizations for effective action, but the vital role that feminist activists play in deepening our theoretical understandings.

Ximena Bunster also nudged me to look beyond militaries to militarism. She tutored me in the process by which many Chilean middle-class and affluent women had internalized militaristic beliefs by convincing themselves that socialist President Salvador Allende threatened their class and gendered security. Ximena was one of the first academics to do scholarly research on the particular gendered presumptions—about feminized purity, feminized shame—that male military personnel wielded when torturing women prisoners.[9] Soon after the fall of Pinochet, Ximena invited me to Santiago, where she and her sister took me on a tour of the junta's torture houses—ordinary middle-class residences scattered around Santiago.

At the same time—in the early 1980s—hundreds of British women were organizing a women's peace camp outside the US military's Cruise missile base near the town of Greenham Common. During damp English winters, women activists camping out in tents debated with each other about the relationships of motherhood to peace, activism to disabilities, militarism to patriarchy. I tried to read everything they wrote. Ximena and the Greenham women convinced me that I would have to explore the ideas about femininities and masculinities to fully explain the micro-processes that nurture militarization. I would have to trace how some women absorbed, while others resisted, the appealing ideas of masculinized protection and feminized patriotism.

Prostitution. Marriage. Rape. I was never taught about any of these at Connecticut College or Berkeley. Now, as I was about to write what became my first feminist-informed book, I had to find ways to explore each of them—and the relationships between them—in societies as different as Chile, Vietnam, China, Nicaragua, Japan, Britain, and the United States. I read Kathleen Barry's and Susan Brownmiller's new, controversial feminist social histories of prostitution and wartime rape.[10] I devoured Myna Trustram's fresh investigation of post-Crimean War British officials' confusion over male soldiers' marrying ("Are wives good for the military's imperial enterprise?") and Judith Walkowitz's analysis of disenfranchised British women's late-nineteenth-century campaigning against the state's draconian regulation of poor women in port towns, designed by the government to protect male sailors from venereal disease.[11]

Researching *Does Khaki Become You?* (1983) convinced me that, though they routinely have denied it, male military strategists have thought—and still think—about women a lot. Chiefly, they worry about women: can they control them so that women—differing by nationality, class, ethnicity, sexuality, age, and race—will play the specific roles that the military strategists need them to play? Not all women are obliging.

I dedicated *Khaki* to my mother. She received the page proof of the dedication in the mail the day before she died.

I had published *Ethnic Soldiers* with Penguin UK (1980). *Khaki* was published first by a small British left-wing press, Pluto. So not only did I consciously compare British and American women's militarizing experiences, I imagined Greenham Common British peace activists picking up a copy—would it ring true to them? *Khaki* was the first of my books to be translated—into Finnish and Swedish. Since then, other of my books have been translated — into Korean, Turkish, Japanese, and, most recently, French. This has constantly reminded me that I have to take conscious steps to overcome the potent parochialism that comes with being an American. It has made me think about diverse readers, readers with their own experiences and urgent concerns: how will this sound to Ayşe, Lepa, Insook, Rela, Ruri, Ailbhe, or Annica?

A few years ago I was sitting with a small group of Kurdish activist women, members of a feminist group KAMER, who were running a women-staffed restaurant in the southeastern besieged Turkish town of Diyarbakır. In their hands were copies—in Turkish—of *Maneuvers* (2000), the book that continued the reflections on the militarization of women's lives and was influenced by reading historian Philippa Levine's eye-opening works.[12] I was awed by these KAMER women activists' deep understanding of what it takes to resist militarizing forces. One Kurdish woman described the dilemma she faced since her family relied on her husband's salary earned as a civilian truck driver for the Turkish military. Another described the deep pride she felt singing beloved Kurdish folk songs once banned by the state, and yet she rejected violence as a means for sustaining Kurdish culture. Still another woman that day said she was committed to ending domestic violence in the Kurdish community, but to pursuing that goal without handing Turkish nationalists a gift with which to denigrate Kurds. When I think today of the sprawling war on the Turkish-Syrian border, I try to imagine very specifically how these Kurdish feminist women are making sense of—and devising strategies to act in—this hydra-headed conflict.

Bananas, Beaches and Bases has recently come out in a new, updated edition (2014). I learned so much doing the research for this new edition: the innovative transnational women's advocacy among banana plantation workers and domestic workers, but also the new structures and strategies devised to sustain patriarchal ideas and practices. *Bananas* had first been published by a small British feminist press, Pandora, in 1989. I wanted to make visible women surviving on the margins of international politics. By giving them the attention they were due, myriad forms of gendered power used to shape the international political system could be revealed—power wielded to promote overseas military bases, tourism industries, brand-name clothing manufacture, and the global trade in tea, mangos, and bananas. To write *Bananas*, I drew on feminist historians' and feminist anthropologists' accounts, as well as analyses by women labor organizers.

Only when the original edition of *Bananas* was about to go to the printers was it taken up for US distribution by the University of California Press. I was reluctant to have it published by a university press, fearing that that would limit its readership to people in academia. Yet having a university press imprint has seemed to provide it with sufficient credibility to be adopted in college courses. This came as quite a surprise to me. *Bananas* has since had a life of its own. Naomi Schneider was the brave UCal editor who first offered to co-print it with Pandora. Naomi and I have gone on to publish six more books together.

Bananas, Beaches and Bases first came out at a time when students and teachers were increasingly eager to test their ideas outside their own societies. The excitement generated by the 1975–85 UN Decade for Women and the follow-up 1995 UN Conference on Women in Beijing, as well as the growing awareness of national women's movements' interdependence across state borders, has added fuel to this globalized gender curiosity.

In 1986, Joni Seager published the first-ever global atlas of women. No one had ever before imagined, much less tried to create, such an atlas, with its forty brightly colored maps. *Women in the World: An International Atlas* enticed readers for the first time to compare divorce rates between the United States, China, and Germany; to wonder why rates of women in paid work, women's access to land titles, and glaringly unequal male and female literacy rates differed so widely between France, Poland, Nigeria, and India.[13] The atlas put American women's lives in an international context so boldly displayed that we couldn't avoid asking worldly questions. The atlas also nudged us to take seriously the patriarchal politics of data: who was bothering to systematically collect what data to reveal the realities of women's lives? In subsequent, new editions, Joni Seager has exposed in equally bright hues the worldwide realities of sex-trafficking routes, rape in war zones, commercial beauty contests, and the creation of battered women's shelters.[14]

Simultaneously, courses and programs investigating the complex workings of masculinities and femininities have proliferated in universities around the world: Seoul's Ewha University, Tokyo's Ochanomizu University, the University of the West Indies, University College Dublin, and the National University of Colombia. Their students and faculty have sought out writings they could build upon, defying conventional disciplinary boundaries.

The surprising career of *Bananas* also has been propelled by feminist stirrings in the long-masculinized discipline of international relations (IR). Ann Tickner's *Gender in International Relations* was published in 1992, spelling out a new feminist theory of international politics. It created a buzz. Already, in 1990, a small conference had been held at Wellesley College to explore why most IR writers and teachers seemed so impervious to the feminist questions and insights that, for a decade, had been reshaping history, literary studies, philosophy, anthropology, and art history. Ann Tickner was a key participant in this gathering, and those conferences, professional association reforms, and new journals and publishers' lists have made a significant dent in IR's masculinist culture.[15] As an academic field, however, IR's gender consciousness remains modest. One only has to count the number of women authors on IR assigned reading lists or look at what counts as "expertise" in current commentaries on Middle East conflicts, Putin's expansionism, or US drone warfare.

Throughout this winding journey, teaching has remained at the core of what I do. Teaching and writing—they are not rivals. They are in constant conversation. For instance, when I tried to open a feminist window onto the Iraq-US war, I first taught about Nimo, a Baghdad woman attempting to sustain her small beauty salon, for two years before I dared to start writing a book in which she helps shed light on that bloody conflict (*Nimo's War, Emma's War*, 2010). Nimo taught me to explore women's paid work before a war breaks out, during its first months, and into the depths of its violence. Gendered economics do not end when the first shot is fired.

I've come to realize that teaching occurs in all sorts of venues—guest lectures, Skyped classes (in Pennsylvania, Lahore...), as well as workshops and radio talk shows. In each teaching venue, varieties of knowledge are at play. I learn as much as I teach.

Last October, I was invited to give a talk in Bogotá by Humanas, a Colombian women's rights group which has been supporting women traumatized by the decades-long civil war and pressuring the Colombian government and insurgent male negotiators meeting in Havana to ensure that immunity not be granted to perpetrators of sexual violence against women, as an allegedly "necessary price for peace."[16] The highway from the airport to downtown Bogotá is lined with glassy new high-rise office buildings, home to mining and banking companies eagerly anticipating the end of the war. The center of Bogatá is thriving, with caravans of buses bringing low-paid workers into the city every morning, many of them women earning their livings by cleaning the expensive new condos now creeping up the Andean hillsides above the smog line. I was uneasy about giving such a talk, since I know so little about the wartime experiences of Colombia's racially diverse and class-stratified women. The audience for the keynote included Afro-Colombian women, local activists from the coast, and displaced women driven out of mountainous rural areas, as well as human rights activists and academics from Bogotá and Medellín. Simultaneous translation enabled non-English speakers to follow the lecture, and, more importantly, to add their own ideas in the discussion that followed.

Colombian women at the meeting wanted to know whether patriarchy could infect peace processes, whether sexual violence was likely to persist after the war, how women could gain land titles if men continued to be imagined as the "real" farmers. I felt as though I was taking part in an intense seminar.

Recently, I have been invited to take part in several gatherings organized by WILPF, the Women's International League for Peace and Freedom. WILPF's dynamic international director, the British feminist international lawyer Madeleine Rees, has drawn me into gatherings in The Hague, Stockholm, Geneva, New York, and Sarajevo. I've been stretched. How could my own work and those of scores of researchers now exploring the messy gendered endings of war and the militarized gendered dynamics of "post-war" societies be of any value to these gritty local and transnational feminist activists? I have had to learn, for instance, about the complicated workings of the United Nations and about transnational feminists' persistent efforts to challenge patriarchal mindsets, institutional priorities, and operational routines. I've had to learn to spot sexism in the workings of the Security Council, the Secretary-General's office, and the Department of Peacekeeping Operations. The feminist puzzles I am now tussling with include: what allows UN officials to claim that their hands are tied when male soldiers deployed on peacekeeping missions engage in sexual abuse of the very people they are deployed to protect? Why did the Vatican delegation vehemently object to the phrase "gender-based violence" appearing in the 2014 Arms Trade Treaty? Then there is the still-glaring absence of women civil society activists at internationally sponsored peace negotiations (explored in Chapter Two of this book), negotiations that will shape women's lives for decades to come. What sustains the myth that "only men with guns can make peace"?

Feminist puzzling never stops. Feminist learning never stops. That is the good news.

CHAPTER EIGHT

Cafeteria Ladies, Wonder Woman at the UN, and Other Acts of Resistance

On November 10, 2016, British women stopped working. Or, rather, they stopped being paid what they were worth for their work. Feminist economists had calculated that, as a result of the multiple processes that perpetuate unequal pay between women and men, from November 10 to December 31 that year, British women were working for free.[1]

Equal pay has been one of the longest-standing demands of most countries' women's movements. It was at the core of Second Wave feminism. Women's access to paid work was integral to most suffrage movements. And that activism reaped reforms: new national laws, new systems of wage accounting, and, perhaps most importantly, new expectations for fairness among women workers. Yet equal pay remains a goal still to be fully realized in virtually every country. According to the Global Gender Gap's 2016 rankings of 144 countries' relative gaps between their own women and men in the combined areas of education, politics, health, and economics, Iceland ranked No. 1 in gender parity. Yemen ranked No. 144.[2]

Yet it is not a question of whether Iceland is relatively affluent and Yemen is desperately poor. Rather, within Iceland, women and men have relatively equal chances of obtaining good health, education, political influence, and economic wellbeing. Within Yemen, while everyone in that war-beleaguered country has to cope with scarce resources, a gap has nonetheless been created between men and women in access to those scarce resources. On the same rankings, Rwanda ranks No.5, the Philippines No.7, whereas more affluent Belgium ranks No.24 and Spain ranks No.29.[3] That is, patriarchy is not just summed up in wealth or poverty. Patriarchy survives by constantly re-entrenching certain gendered beliefs, values, and relationships. A country that becomes more affluent is not necessarily a country that becomes less prone to privileging certain forms of masculinity over all forms of femininity.

To rank how countries were doing in 2016 in closing their economic gaps between men and women, the Global Gender Gap researchers examined five measurable dimensions of each country's gendered economy: paid labor force participation, wage equality for similar work, earned income, proportions of male and female workers in managerial posts, and proportions of male and female workers holding professional and technical positions. The UK ranked a less-than-stellar 26th. If only "wage equality for similar work" were taken into account, the UK's gender gap would rank even lower: 66th. It is not clear if the UK's withdrawal from the European Union will widen these gaps further. If it makes Britons any less embarrassed, the United States ranked below it on the 2016 overall economic gender gap scale, at No.53. The US ranking on just the measure of gender gap in "wage equality for similar work," however, was higher than Britain's. This, too, was before any impacts of the Trump presidency on workplace fairness could be felt.

The gap between women's paid work and men's paid work is shaped by globalized patriarchy—companies scouring the planet for places where they can cheapen women's work; national governments competing to lure profit-maximizing company executives by offering up their own women as "cheaper" than their neighbors'; consumers demanding the lowest possible prices for goods without caring much about the lives of the workers in other countries who made those goods.

Yet globalization is not the only patriarchal process at work today that is sustaining the gaps between what men earn and what women earn. Unequal pay is perpetuated by local, even intimate, patriarchies: ideas about marriage; presumptions about skill; zero-sum thinking among workmates; practices of childcare and eldercare; whose voices are heard; whose ideas are taken seriously. One should never imagine that critiquing globalized capitalism's flaws, as deep as they can be, by itself will either reveal or tackle the full workings of patriarchy.

Everett is not the sort of town that one looks to for major resistances to patriarchy.

When most people think of greater Boston, they think of higher education powerhouses such as Harvard, MIT, and Wellesley; they picture iconic places such as Fenway Park, home of the beloved Red Sox; they imagine ethnically diverse café patrons drinking lattes as they stare at their Apple laptops. But that is only the tip of greater Boston's proverbial iceberg. Like greater London, Paris, or Tokyo, greater Boston comprises neighborhoods and towns, each with its own local character, its own globalized history, and its own ongoing gendered dynamics.[4]

Everett faces downtown Boston's skyline from across the Mystic River. The river has been polluted for decades by chemical company operations. A small, working-class city (population:

43,885), Everett is equipped with its own governing authority, yet is affected by the changing currents of the larger metropolitan region. The town has been growing, its residents becoming more racially and ethnically diverse: by 2015, Latinos made up 21.5 percent of Everett's population, while African Americans and Blacks (mostly people of Afro-Caribbean heritage) together comprised 18.9 percent of the town's residents.[5]

In 2015, both Everett's men's and women's median annual income levels were lower than those of either Massachusetts or the nation. Yet within the town there was a notable gender income gap: Everett men's median annual earnings were $32,343, whereas its women's annual median earnings were just $24,576. Everett had a gender income gap of 18 percent.[6] This economic inequality took on added significance in light of the fact that almost a third (30.5 percent) of all of the town's households were headed by women. This proportion was higher than the 20 percent of all households that were women-headed in both Massachusetts and the nation.[7]

Dorothy Simonelli had earned her income working for two decades as a food server in Everett's public schools. In local parlance, she was a "lunch lady."[8] She and her cafeteria co-workers had not set out to challenge patriarchy. What they wanted was equal pay with their male school co-workers. Virtually all of the food servers were women. Over the generations, school cafeteria work had become feminized—thus "lunch ladies." It was the sort of job—along with work in child care and elder care, work as a waitress, seamstress, electronics assembler, industrial food processor, tea-picker, domestic cleaner, nurse's aide, or secretary —which patriarchal employers (and their investors) believed deserved low pay precisely because it was done chiefly by women. Twin patriarchal values and beliefs underpin these low wages paid to employees in feminized jobs: anything done chiefly by women is not worth much; and, if it *were* a job worth much, it would be done by men.

Everett's lunch ladies were dependent on their jobs to support their families and had little history of political organizing. So it took courage for these women to challenge such widely held patriarchal beliefs. Yet, back in the late 1980s, Dorothy Simonelli and forty other Everett lunch ladies had joined a union, Local 26 of the Hotel and Food Workers Union. They began talking among themselves about the difference they noticed in their paychecks compared to those received by the town's school custodians.

Politicization often starts with making comparisons—and then wondering what causes the differences that one discovers. Among the common discoveries are one's employers' patriarchal assumptions and policies that do not match the daily realities of the job. "School custodian" in many towns was, in the 1980s—and still is—a masculinized job category. As such, employers—including the town's patriarchal officials—deemed it a job worthy of higher pay than for feminized cafeteria work. Being a janitor was allegedly more skilled than preparing and serving lunch to children. On top of that, because they were performing a "manly" job, custodians' pay allegedly provided financial support to household heads.

This presumed difference did not jibe with the lunch ladies' own understandings of their daily reality. Marilyn Jancsy, the lunch ladies' lead plaintiff in what became their equal pay court case, explained to the judges: as routine parts of her cafeteria work, she "cleaned and scrubbed, and lifted heavy objects such as ten-pound logs of frozen hamburger and forty-pound cases of tomatoes." Dorothy Simonelli recalled, "Let me tell you, when you go home and fall asleep at the table, it was work.... We worked hard, and we deserved more."[9]

When the Everett lunch ladies found that they were making only half as much as the men working as the town's public school custodians, they were motivated to act. In 1989 forty-one lunch ladies filed suit in Massachusetts state court, claiming that this pay inequity violated the state's equal pay law.

They won. The lower court judge awarded the lunch ladies $1 million in back-pay.

Then they lost. The Everett School Committee appealed to the Massachusetts Supreme Judicial Court. It took another ten years for the town officials' appeal to be heard. In 1998 the SJC judges decided, in a 4–3 split, in favor of the town authorities. The four-judge majority ruled that cafeteria work and custodial work were not the same, could not be compared, and thus the state's 1945 equal pay law did not apply.

But losing a court case was not the end of this story of local resistance to patriarchy. It takes extraordinary stamina—and long lifespans—to effectively challenge adaptable, modernizable patriarchy. It also takes the crafting of fresh concepts and feminist-informed gender transformations of institutions.

First, concepts. "Equal pay for equal work" may have sounded progressive when the state lawmakers in Massachusetts and other states along with national governments passed the equal pay laws. Equality, though, is not synonymous with *equity*. In practice, the concept of equality did not upset adaptable patriarchy precisely because so many women were being channeled by employers (and schools and parents) into feminized jobs—into jobs where the majority of people doing that work were women. This patriarchal channeling allowed the worth of those employees' work, and of the skills needed to perform that work, to be perpetually denigrated.

Who is formally categorized as a "skilled worker" and who gets to define what work is "skilled"—together, these are two crucial gears in the machinery of any patriarchal workplace. Those gears only keep turning if they are continuously re-oiled with re-enforced patriarchal ideas. To be dismissed as doing "what women naturally do" is to be dismissed as not-skilled. A skill is not "natural," however; a skill is something one has to be trained for, not something that comes with the gendered territory. Being characterized as an "unskilled" worker has denied women workers fair pay in a wide range of industries around the world.

Beyond pay, though, in the minds of many women workers, the designations of "unskilled" or "semi-skilled" have deprived them of the respect they were due. A fight over what counts as a "skill" was evident in the Everett lunch ladies' court testimonies. It had echoed a nationally celebrated protest in England a decade earlier. The collective walkout by British women workers at the Dagenham Ford factory was fueled by anger over unfair job categorization, as well as the resultant low pay. These women factory workers stitched the seats that went into Ford's cars and trucks. They knew it took skills to perform this work well. One is not born knowing how to do heavy, complex stitching. It was on the demand that their work be upgraded to "skilled" that the plant's women stitchers went out on strike in 1968.[10]

Patriarchy is sustained by those co-workers who withhold their valuable support for women colleagues because they see the world as a zero-sum universe: you gain, I lose. If you are a man doing work that not only your employer but you yourself imagines to be skilled, you might resent those women co-workers doing cafeteria work or stitching car seats when they claim that they are as skilled as you are. The widespread internalization of this patriarchal resentment (and accompanying fear) has subverted potential male/female alliances in workplaces as different as automobile assembly plants and public schools.[11]

Consequently, to challenge workplace patriarchy, a new feminist concept was needed: comparable worth. This went beyond mere equality. This addressed justice—that is, equity.

Concepts matter. A poor choice of concept can reinforce distortions in our understandings of the world and our place in it. But reliably useful concepts can provide us with 20-20 vision of complex realities. Concepts, therefore, are not merely abstractions. They have consequences. They can galvanize. They can inspire pushback. To campaign for "equal pay for comparable work" was to offer a fresh concept that provided a fresh goal, enabling women in diverse workplaces to challenge the patriarchal assumption that one cannot make reliable comparisons between the work done by men and the work done by women. "Comparable worth" subverted the patriarchal assertion that work done mainly by men is inherently worth more than work done mainly by women.

Secondly, institutions. Changing concepts mattered for the lunch ladies' campaign, but so did changing institutions. It took more than twenty-five years for the Everett campaign to change Massachusetts public policy. Increasing women's voices in the Massachusetts state legislature had to be achieved as well.

While Massachusetts is popularly imagined to be a solidly Democratic state (a "blue" state) in its usual electoral preferences, for generations it had been a patriarchal Democratic Party organization that dominated state and local politics. The gendered history of Massachusetts state party politics reminds us that being "liberal" does not automatically inoculate a society against patriarchy. For instance, when the Everett lunch ladies brought their suit in 1989, women made up less than 20 percent of the Massachusetts state legislature. There had never been a woman governor. The state's national Congressional delegation was routinely masculinized.[12] By 2016, there were some signs of a rollback of those masculinized Massachusetts state Democratic Party and state legislative cultures. Democratic women had sought and won more elective offices. They now comprised 26 percent of the state legislature. This did not put Massachusetts far out in front of most states (the 2016 US national average for women in state legislatures was just 24.8 percent). Nevertheless, this increase did have an impact on what legislators deemed an issue, what they considered worthy of expending their political capital on, and what sorts of alliances they formed in order to achieve the enactment of new laws.

It was not, however, simply a matter of numbers. It was that many of these new state women legislators entered office with a feminist awareness of women's economic realities. One such Massachusetts state legislator was Patricia Jehlen. She had begun her political career in the town of Somerville, another mainly working-class town within the larger Boston metropolitan region. Having built an electoral base in Somerville, Jehlen ran as a Democrat and won a seat in the state's lower house, and then later in the state's Senate. It was as a Massachusetts state senator that Pat Jehlen played a crucial role in reviving the question of pay equity for the Everett lunch ladies.[13]

After the Massachusetts Supreme Judicial Court ruled against the Everett lunch ladies, Pat Jehlen introduced a bill to revise the state's equal pay laws so that their enforcement took account of "comparable worth." She introduced the bill every session for seventeen years. Every session the bill died.

In 2014, Pat Jehlen tried a new strategy. She made common cause with fellow legislator Ellen Story, from western Massachusetts. First, their new bill offered a clear definition of comparable worth as a yardstick for pay equity, enabling comparisons to be made between the pay of jobs that are similar even if they have different titles. Secondly, they added a provision that protected employers against potential sex discrimination lawsuits if they could demonstrate that they conducted regular salary reviews and show that they had made bona fide efforts to address wage disparities in their workplaces. Thirdly, and most newsworthily, Jehlen and Story inserted a provision that made it illegal for employers to ask prospective employees their pay in their former job. Asking this question for years had encouraged employers to peg women's starting pay at a lower level than newly hired men.[14]

By 2014, the chair of the state Senate's powerful Ways and Means Committee had been taken over by another woman legislator. She signed on to the bill's supportive alliance. The office of Massachusetts state Attorney General had been won by another feminist-informed woman, Maura Healey. Her office was responsible for enforcing labor laws. She helped persuade the state's business leaders that the Jehlen-Story bill was fair and in their own ultimate interest. In 2016, the pay equity bill passed both houses of the Massachusetts state legislature unanimously. Its passage became national news. According to the *New York Times*, "Massachusetts has become the first state to bar employers from asking about applicants' salaries before offering them a job."[15]

When it was signed into law in August 2016 by the Republican governor, among the people invited to the event was Dorothy Simonelli. She had not wanted to come. She was by then in her eighties. She told friends that, after so many years of fighting for fair pay, she was worn out. By now, all of the other Everett lunch ladies who had brought that historic suit back in 1989 had died. Her family members finally persuaded her to attend the signing of the pay equity bill into law, convincing her she would be doing it for her grandchildren. When asked to speak at the event, Dorothy Simonelli was brief: "I have ten grandchildren—five boys and five girls. ... This is for them and all future women in the workplace. R-E-S-P-E-C-T."[16]

Women whose workplace is the United Nations Secretariat building, the glass-wrapped high-rise overlooking Manhattan on one side and the East River on the other, may seem a planet away from the lunch ladies of Everett. And in many ways they are. Their clients are governments, not teenagers. Their daily work rarely involves lifting ten-pound logs of hamburger meat. Yet in 2016, many of these women working as international civil servants decided the time had come for unconventional joint action. Their goal was not a pay rise; it was overturning what they believed was an officially selected patriarchal symbol: Wonder Woman.

Working inside the behemoth that the United Nations has become requires a lot of stamina. One has to have a high tolerance for prolonged processes, complex decision-making, multiple actors, rival objectives, and uncertain support. The mix of parochial self-interests and lofty ideals is at the very core of the United Nations. So is patriarchy.

Despite the early influence of such forceful women as Eleanor Roosevelt and Vijaya Lakshmi Pandit, the United Nations, from its launch out of the ashes of World War II, was dominated not just by men, but by patriarchal assumptions about states, war, peace, power, security, expertise, economic development, and human rights.[17] As is true of most patriarchal institutions, this does not mean that there were not women working inside it. Even the most masculinity-privileging institutions depend on women as clerical workers, cleaners, cafeteria workers, and unpaid child-caring spouses. Sometimes these women complied with its patriarchal cultural expectations; sometimes they tried to subvert them.

Most women inside the UN have held jobs in its international civil service. Educated women from scores of member countries gained work as secretaries, accountants, archivists, travel planners, web designers, statisticians, international lawyers, program officers, field workers—all the sorts of jobs it takes to keep the wheels of such a large transnational organization turning. They have worked in Rome for the Food and Agriculture Organization, in Geneva for the International Labour Organization, for the

World Health Organization, for the UN High Commissioner for Refugees, and for the UN Human Rights Council. They have worked in The Hague at the International Criminal Court, in Paris for the UN Educational, Scientific and Cultural Organization (UNESCO), and in Nairobi for the UN Environment Program.

The greatest concentration of UN civil servants, however, has worked in New York City, at the UN's official headquarters. The UN General Assembly meets in New York, bringing together government-appointed delegates of all 193 member-states (the newest members being Timor-Leste, Montenegro, and South Sudan). The home of the Security Council (dominated by the "P5," the delegates of its five permanent member states—the United States, the United Kingdom, China, Russia, and France— each wielding veto power) is also in New York. So too is the UN Secretariat, the vertical workplace of most of the UN's civil servants. This means that in New York also is the office of the UN Secretary-General, the person chosen by the member states to globally represent the entire organization.

UN civil service work can often be bureaucratically numbing. Yet gaining a UN civil service post is very attractive, given its relative benefits, security, pay, and social status. Whenever one of the Secretariat's 41,000 jobs opens up, there are on average 200 applicants for the post.[18] As in most complex modern organizations, positions in the UN Secretariat are ranked in a steep hierarchy, and it is those occupying the senior posts who wield dispropor-tionate influence over what questions are taken seriously, how scarce resources are spent, which organizational mandates will be fulfilled, and which will be treated as mere window-dressing.

At the 1995 Beijing Decade+10 UN meeting on women, the UN's state members approved the Beijing Platform for Action. One of its provisions was for women and men to reach parity in the UN's senior posts by 2000. That benchmark date has come and gone. Men continue to fill the majority of the UN Secretariat's senior posts. For instance, in 2012, a dozen years after the Beijing Platform's commitment, women filled a majority (70.6 percent) of the UN employees at the lowest level, P-1. By stark contrast, women filled only 24.0 percent of senior directors' posts, ranked D-2.[19] Looking further into the higher ranks, where even more influence is wielded, the patriarchal picture is all the more clear: in 2015, six undersecretaries-general, senior appointive posts, resigned. All were women. All of the six were replaced by men. At the next level down from this—assistant secretaries-general, still very senior—men comprised 77 percent of the occupants.[20]

To assess how patriarchal any group is, and to develop an effective strategy to transform that group's outlook and practice, one has to do some organizational sleuthing. Feminist detective work requires learning about both the organization's formal hierarchy and the day-to-day decision-making routines. Some crucial decisions are not made at the very top. Then, with this information in hand, one needs to find out where the women are and where the men are. One needs to ask if certain men—by race, nationality, sexuality, career path, expertise—are more likely to get promoted, to be tapped for influential posts. And, of course, the feminist sleuth asks who are the promoters, who are the appointers—and who chooses *them*?

An organizational snapshot, though, will not suffice. To track and challenge any organization's patriarchy over the long haul, one will have to keep gathering this essential information, again and then again. That is because part of the formula for sustaining patriarchy has been to shift influence away from certain seemingly prized posts after women with intersectional feminist commitments gain access to them.

Almost from its start in 1945, the UN was criticized by women's advocates for operating in ways that privileged certain sorts of masculinity and masculinized ways of doing business. It was chastised as well as for operating in the world as if women's rights, conditions and ideas were secondary, if worth paying attention to at all. These criticisms came from women working within their own government's UN delegations, from women working as UN staffers, and from women active in a multiplying number of diverse feminist and human rights NGOs.

The responses to these criticisms have been ongoing and multiple, precisely because patriarchy has been so "sustainable," so able to adjust without actually surrendering. The initial response came early in the UN's existence: the UN Commission on the Status of Women (CSW) was created in 1946. Every March, civil society women activists from around the world convene in New York (if they can obtain US entry visas) to lobby the CSW. They attempt to expand the commitments of the CSW or, as is often the case, try to defend the commitments made the year before from conservative push-back. Every year particular governments maneuver to prevent the expansion of those gender commitments. In recent years, the Putin-led Russian government has joined with the Vatican and other conservative states' delegations—for instance, those of Uganda, Malaysia, and Saudi Arabia—to shrink international commitments to women's rights and gender equity. They claim that such commitments undermine states' sovereignty or violate the sanctity of the family—or both. The European Union's member states' delegations, together with those of Canada, Norway, and Iceland, have been among those on whom civil society feminists have most relied to counter these patriarchal moves.

During the Obama administration (2009–17), US delegates had been strong allies for women's advocates. Under the Trump administration, however, the US delegation seemed to switch sides in UN gender negotiations. Transnational feminist advocates watched with alarm as, in January 2017, the Trump administration's first international policy move was to reimpose the so-called "global gag rule." Formally known as the "Mexico City policy," it banned US government foreign aid to any organization, for instance a local health clinic in Senegal, offering abortion services or the full range of reproductive health counseling. Under the Trump administration's expanded interpretation, the US global gag rule ban was not just reimposed, it was extended. As of January 2017, the ban on US foreign aid extended to any organization or clinic that received any of its own funding from any donor who, even elsewhere, provided these crucial reproductive health services.[21] Women's advocates focusing on the annual CSW negotiations predicted that the US delegation's support hereafter would be tepid at best, backing the conservative states at worst. No areas of UN commitment have been more contentious, in these behind-closed-doors, inter-state CSW annual negotiations, than women's reproductive rights and LGBTQ rights.[22]

After the creation of the CSW came "the Decade." Responding to pressures from the international women's movement activists, in the early 1970s the UN created the UN Decade for Women: 1975– 85. It was intended to ensure that women—their ideas, experiences, needs, and aspirations—were fully incorporated into all global and local development efforts. For many local women activists, taking part in one of the UN Decade's large and lively meetings was their first chance to influence the distant UN and to experience having their own stake in challenging its patriarchal routines.

During the Decade, in 1979, the UN General Assembly passed the Convention for the Elimination of Discrimination Against Women (CEDAW). By 2013, 187 of the UN's 193 member governments had signed and ratified (if not always implemented) CEDAW. Even when governments failed to live up to their commitments under CEDAW, their ratifications empowered local women's groups to hold up CEDAW as a standard for public policy and practice. Among those governments whose officials continued to refuse to sign and ratify CEDAW have been Tonga, Iran, Somalia, Sudan, and the United States.[23]

In a major political breakthrough, a coalition of women's advocates inside and outside the UN did the research to underpin and then draft, and persuaded the fifteen members of the UN Security Council to pass, a resolution acknowledging women's distinctive experiences of and perspectives on war. In October 2000, the Council passed UN Security Council Resolution 1325 on Women, Peace and Security. For the first time, the masculinized Security Council—where major issues of international security are debated and acted upon—committed not only its members but all of the UN's agencies and all of its member states to explicitly consider the ideas, interests, and experiences of women in resolving armed conflicts and in the crucial steps toward rebuilding societies in the wake of collective violence.

Resolution 1325 was designed, by those women activists who were central to its theorizing and its lobbying, to commit governments and agencies to pay particular attention to the abuses and the losses women suffered in wars (for example, to stop imagining that rape was merely a form of inevitable wartime "collateral damage"). Its reasoning went further: 1325 acknowledged women as more than silent victims. The resolution committed member states and UN officials to roll back patriarchal ways of conducting the international business of war-ending and peace-building by including women (especially women active in civil society organizations in war zones) and their ideas in both formal peace negotiations and post-war operations.

The human rights, women's rights and feminist peace groups that were in the forefront of persuading the fifteen state delegates on the Security Council to pass 1325 were experienced in the patriarchal practice of "pass and shelve." So they pressed members of the Security Council to pass successive resolutions, each intended to close the loopholes or sharpen the intentions of 1325. They also created a monitoring group—the NGO Working Group on Women, Peace and Security—to hold both member states and the UN Secretariat accountable for their implementations of 1325. Among the Working Group's members today are Women's International League for Peace and Freedom (WILPF), Nobel Women's Initiative, Care International, MADRE, Human Rights Watch, International Alert, the Consortium for Gender, Security, and Human Rights, and Refugees International.[24]

What is striking when one tracks this gendered history of the United Nations is women's advocates' constant need to update their organizational and lobbying strategies just to keep up with the UN masculinizers' own perpetual updating maneuvers. 1946, 1975, 1979, 1995, 2000—each has marked a fresh attempt by women's advocates to checkmate the masculinizers. The process is far from over. The updating of patriarchy has not reached its end.

In 2010, again at the initiative of transnational feminist activists who had been pushing against and tugging at the UN's patriarchal system, a new UN agency was authorized by the member states of the General Assembly: UN Women. It was designed to have higher status and greater authority, together with a wider mandate, than the several existing units within the UN system which had been responsible for ensuring that the realities, needs, and ideas of women were taken seriously—not only in matters of peace and war, but in terms of the decisions and the data collection that were shaping international policies concerning health, sexuality, weapons trade, economic development, law, policing, and the environment.[25] But the hard-working staff people inside UN Women routinely see their programs underfunded (especially when measured against their far-reaching global mandate). Their experts are often ignored when major decisions are made, or they are "let into the room" only if they don't demand "too much."

One has to develop a feminist hawk-eye to see opportunities for entrenching women's rights in international agreements and to prevent subversions of those rights in the vast UN arena. Transnational feminists have counted among their victories the getting of "gender-based violence" into the 2013 innovative Arms Trade Treaty. Their "Make It Binding" campaign persuaded the treaty-writers to include the use of firearms in gender-based violence as one of the new binding treaty criteria for prohibiting weapons exports.[26] Likewise, in 2015, an alliance of feminist activists, UN insiders, and feminist-friendly government delegates successfully persuaded governments to make "gender equality" one of the UN's explicit sustainable development goals (SDGs). "Achieve gender equality and empower all women and girls" became one of the seventeen agreed-upon collective objectives: SDG 5.[27] It has taken concerted campaigns to achieve these recent victories precisely because so many governments have opposed them.

Every feminist policy success within the UN system has been a struggle. Every success, nevertheless, has improved the actual lives of millions of women only in so far as that policy has been sustained over time and effectively implemented. Achieving this demands even more feminist activism.

Among the most difficult of the recent challenges has been to persuade member states to elect a woman to serve as the UN Secretary-General (SG). The term of Korean diplomat Ban Ki-moon as Secretary-General was due to end in December 2016. The unwritten convention observed by UN member states was to circulate the post of SG among geographic regions of the world.

In 2016 it was presumably Eastern Europe's "turn." It was the turn, that is, of a senior male diplomat or senior male member state's government official. In the UN's seventy-one-year history, only men had ever served in the organization's highest post. They were diverse men—from Norway, Sweden, the UK, Egypt, Peru, South Korea, Austria, Ghana—but they shared presumably patriarchal credentials, a masculinized expertise, trustworthiness (in the eyes of other men), and alleged gravitas. No woman had ever been deemed to possess these attributes in sufficient supply to earn the votes of the Security Council's rotating and permanent member states, especially not the decisive votes of the Security Council's powerful P5.

For over a year, through the summer and into the fall of 2016, feminists inside the UN and in the scores of civil society groups outside strategized, coordinated, and crafted alliances with friendly governments, all aimed at having a woman elected to succeed Ban Ki-moon as Secretary-General. It was time. It was long past time. To achieve this goal, however, these UN-focused activists knew they would have to make the selection process more open than it typically had been in the past. A more transparent SG selection process, they calculated, would have a better chance of weakening the hold on the selection process of the institution's masculinized bargaining culture. In this, they succeeded. In 2016, for the first time in the UN's seven-decade history, there were public, televised presentations by the twelve top SG candidates. For the first time, too, half of the candidates interviewed were women, each with impressive foreign policy and international career experience. The six included one from New Zealand (which counts as "European" in UN geopolitical imagining), and two from Eastern Europe. During their interviews, though, only one, Croatia's foreign minister, identified herself as a feminist.

In the end, the members of the Security Council, with all five of the Permanent Members on board, chose another man, Portuguese diplomat António Guterres. He was respected for his leadership of the organization's refugee agency, UNHCR. After being sworn into the post in December, 2016, Secretary-General Guterres promised to listen to women, to take immediate steps to achieve gender parity in senior appointments, and to effectively address the sexual abuse of local women by male peacekeeping soldiers. Feminists welcomed these pledges. They noted at the same time, however, that the masculinization of the UN leadership had been perpetuated.[28]

Enter Wonder Woman.

In the fall of 2016, staff members of the UN's Department of Public Information were looking for a symbol of women's and girls' empowerment.[29] This would be their special contribution to fulfilling the new SDG 5 commitment. Under the UN's current guidelines, though, they were encouraged to craft "partnerships" with private companies. Being public relations professionals, they also were eager to find a symbol that would be eye-catching and a hit on global social media. No actual, living girl or woman seemed to fit the bill.

It is not clear how widely the DPI's staff members consulted with other people in the UN—for instance, UN Women staffers— about the wisdom of their choice. Nor is it clear, even if they did seek advice from gender experts, whether they took it seriously.

What is clear is that they were not ready for the resistance.

Within days of the announcement of the choice of DC Comics' cartoon character Wonder Woman as the UN's special "honorary ambassador" for girls' and women's empowerment, rumbles of dissent began to sound in unusual quarters. Many UN staff in diverse offices—those international civil servants known chiefly for their political caution and organizational discretion—were outraged. In a rare move, they began circulating a petition of dissent addressed to the Secretary-General, first along the corridors of the Secretariat, and then online. They titled it "Reconsider the Choice of Honorary Ambassador for the Empowerment of Women and Girls." By mid-October, 600 staff people had signed the petition.[30] The petitioners took the DPI to task for making such an "inappropriate" and "insensitive" choice:

> Wonder Woman was created 75 years ago. Although the original creators may have intended Wonder Woman to represent a strong and independent "warrior" woman with a feminist message, the reality is that the character's current iteration is that of a large breasted, white woman of impossible proportions, scantily clad in a shimmery, thigh-baring body suit with an American flag motif and knee high boots—the epitome of a "pin-up" girl. [31]

Perhaps these very attributes were what appealed to the DPI staff people. Wonder Woman was not fusty and dusty. She wasn't an innocent. She had a patina of feminized militarism. In fact, she was originally marketed in the United States during World War II as a symbol of American patriotism. Along with Superman and Captain America, she fought the fascists.

Wonder Woman's storyline, if not her big-breasted image, was inspired at the outset in part by women who had been suffragists. It was they who inspired Wonder Woman's exclamation, "Suffering Sappho!" But, as feminist historian Jill Lepore recently revealed, the influence of these women was kept secret during their lives. It was a man, William Moulton Marston, who received credit for having created Wonder Woman, and Marston's relationships with women and attitudes toward both women and femininity were complicated at best.[32]

Like so many fictional women characters, Wonder Woman had a life of her own in the minds of her female fans. For many

American girls and young women who read her 1940s comic books or watched her on 1970s television, Wonder Woman became not a male-invented fantasy, nor a mere vehicle for mobilizing a government's war effort. Rather, with her high spirits, her pursuit of justice, and her golden lasso, she became a symbol of unconventional, if feminized, energy and power. It was women with this understanding of Wonder Woman who chose her as the image for the 1972 debut issue of their new feminist magazine, *Ms.*[33]

But 2016 was not 1972. The United Nations was not the US. Women working as international civil servants were not girls consuming American popular culture. And promoting girls' and women's empowerment across nations and cultures was not the same as mobilizing patriotic militarism. The DPI staff members seemed to have missed these salient differences. Many of the UN women staffers who circulated and signed the petition, however, were keenly aware of them. Moreover, the DPI apparently did not take into account the specific UN gendered context in which they would be announcing their choice of a comic book character as a global ambassador for women's and girls' empowerment. Revelations of male UN peacekeepers abusing local girls and women in the war zones, where they were supposed to be providing protection, and their superiors' apparent complicity in covering up those abuses, had recently rocked the organization. And an explicit commitment of the UN to gender equality had been far from automatic in the 2015 political negotiations. SDG 5 had not slid easily into the organization's Sustainable Development Goals; it had had to be fought for. UN women staffers knew that.

On top of this came the Secretary-General selection contest. Fall 2016 was a moment when many women inside the UN still were smarting from the selection of yet another man to become their new boss. The very transparency of that elite selection process had perhaps heightened many women staffers' awareness of the still-masculinized institutional culture in which they worked. Particularly galling to women working as professionals in the Secretariat may have been the placement of life-size cut-outs of Wonder Woman in the headquarters lobby, where they had to see them every day as they headed for the elevators and up to their offices.

The staff women's petition continued:

> It is alarming that the United Nations would consider using a character with an *overtly sexualized image* at a time when the headline news in the United States and the world is the objectification of women and girls....
>
> The bottom line appears to be that the United Nations was unable to find a real life woman that would be able to champion the rights of ALL women on the issue of gender equality and the fight for their empowerment....
>
> Having strong (living, breathing) female role models is a critical aspect of the goal of empowerment of women and girls....
>
> This role is too important to be championed by a "mascot." [34]

The UN's senior officials chose not to heed the petitioners. They went ahead with their press conference, featuring TV and film stars and the head of DC Comics. For the American entertainment company the UN choice dovetailed with their own celebration of Wonder Woman's 75th anniversary and the issuance by the US Postal Service of a commemorative stamp.

The public ceremony at the UN on October 21, 2016 became a stage for the next extraordinary insiders' protest. A multinational, multi-racial group of staff women and men held a protest in the UN headquarters' main lobby. When told by superiors that they could not protest inside the press conference room itself, many of them went inside, stood at the very back of the room and turned their backs on the proceedings. Rows of women with their backs turned on UN officials, actors, and media executives raised their right arms in silent, fisted protest.[35] No one could remember anything like this ever happening inside the UN headquarters before.

Patriarchy works in multiple ways. The UN officials forged ahead with their Wonder Woman campaign, seemingly dismissing as meaningless the staff women's petition and back-turning protest. But Wonder Woman's ambassadorship did not last for long. After a mere two months on the job, the cartoon character was "retired." The UN officials who brought her ambassadorship to an abrupt end in mid-December 2016 denied that the brevity of her tour had anything to do with the in-house critiques and extraordinary public demonstrations by women staff members and their male allies.[36] Yet that is indeed one of the hallmarks of "sustainable" patriarchy. Patriarchal people do occasionally learn from their gendered mistakes, but they rarely admit it. Rather, they reverse, while making it appear that they never succumbed to critical pressure, especially pressure exerted by feminist-informed women. In fact, part of patriarchal people's learning ritual seems to be learning how to deny that they have ever learned anything from anyone but themselves.

Feminist stamina, research, analysis, concept-refining, fund-raising, listening, humor, global-local intersectional networking, alliance-forging, and attentiveness—it is a daunting combination. Yet creating and sustaining this combination is what it takes to resist patriarchy, to stop both its local and international beliefs and practices in their tracks. It is what it takes to prevent patriarchy from succeeding in its perpetual efforts at adaptation.

Updated Patriarchy Is Not Invincible

Women marched through Bogotá, drumming in the rain, to remember the women killed in Colombia's long civil war and to demand that the new peace agreement's promise of gender equity be fulfilled. In Istanbul, they defied state oppression to write "Stronger Together" on posters in nineteen languages. They held a London vigil at the foot of Edith Cavell's statue to express solidarity with refugee women. In the center of Gothenburg, Swedish women sang a rousing version of the new women's anthem "I Won't Keep Quiet," as snow fell on a sea of pink pussy hats.

This was International Women's Day, March 8, 2017.

Together, women and their male and transgender allies around the world were tilting some of the key pillars designed to sustain patriarchy:

- the belief that a lasting peace can be built without guaranteeing women's rights;
- the pressure exerted on women and girls to stay silent—about their experiences of harassment, assault, marginalization, and humiliation;

- the practice of shrinking the space for civil society, where so much of women's political life is lived;
- the dynamic that keeps women divided from each other— by race, by nationality, by sexuality, or by level of security.

Patriarchy may have succeeded in perpetuating itself, but it is not invincible. In fact, one of the questionable beliefs that has sustained patriarchy over generations is precisely the notion that it is immune to challenge, that it will "always be with us." Sometimes that belief is dressed up in stylishly sophisticated garb: it is a sign of supposed worldly maturity to accept that privileging assorted masculinities is an inevitable element of the human condition. The sustaining corollary: thinking that patriarchy can be effectively uprooted is naïve. And, of course, to be naïve is to be feminized.

The feminist beliefs that have informed this book are quite different: that patriarchy is human-made, therefore is vulnerable to challenge. If patriarchy demands constant work of renewal, then patriarchy-sustaining work can be resisted. Absorbing these feminist beliefs enables one to reject resignation in the face of patriarchy's continuing inequities.

To realize that patriarchy requires perpetual restyling and relegitimizing is downright energizing. It fires each of us up to be on the lookout constantly for these patriarchal updating efforts. This attentive feminist stance can make us immune to the patriarchal assumption that the new is always liberating.

The beneficiaries of patriarchy have had to repeatedly update, restyle, and modernize its web of distinctive beliefs, values, and relationships because that web has been so often shredded by feminists and their allies. *When* New Zealand women first won the right to vote, *when* British women won the right to keep control of their property after marriage, *when* Chinese women won the right to divorce, *when* Iraqi women won the right to keep custody of their children after divorce, *when* Palestinian, Egyptian, and Algerian feminists declared that anti-colonial nationalism could not justify the re-entrenchment of men's domination of family or public affairs, *when* Icelandic women called a nationwide strike for gender equality, *when* Rwandan women won the right to inherit their husband's property, *when* Turkish women persuaded judges that a woman beaten by her husband was the victim of a crime, *when* Indian women convinced reporters and editors to treat rape as an outrage, not a cause for shame, *when* American women successfully demanded that workplace sexual abuse be recognized as a violation of an employee's labor rights, *when* a transnational alliance of domestic workers successfully lobbied the International Labour Organization to declare that paid domestic workers had labor rights, *when* South African anti-apartheid women activists compelled their fellow anti-racists to acknowledge the self-serving dynamic between racism and sexism, *when* a transnational network of feminist environmentalists revealed the ways that distorted notions of masculinity were among the significant causes of climate change, *when* Liberian women mobilized to force male war lords to negotiate a peace agreement, *when* Korean women educated us all to replace the misleading term "comfort women" with the more accurate term "sex slaves," *when* Bosnian women and their allies persuaded treaty-writers to define systematic rape as an internationally prosecutable war crime—when every one of these activist successes was achieved, relationships between women and men and the state had to be restructured. Each achievement compelled not just elites but ordinary people to rethink their established assumptions about how societies function. Each accomplishment upset dominant gendered values.

No single one of these notable successes alone has toppled patriarchy. Even all together, these achievements have not pushed Humpty Dumpty permanently off his patriarchal wall.

Individually and collectively, however, these feminist-driven transformations have forced the beneficiaries of patriarchy—and these are diverse, multiple, and often each other's rivals—to devise new strategies, often more fragile, for sustaining that complex system of masculinizing privilege. For instance, some of patriarchy's admirers have promoted women to be television news anchors, but reduced the role to more of a mouthpiece/presenter than a journalist, and insisted that those women squeeze into a narrow mould of feminized "beauty." Others have claimed to be promoting "girl power" by encouraging young women to aspire to be senior corporate executives. Still others have responded to women's workplace strikes by acknowledging women's labor rights, but have then proceeded to craft new employment contracts that require workplace discrimination charges to be settled through out-of-court arbitration—a legal process that favors employers. Still other beneficiaries of patriarchy have opened the doors of science a crack to admit a trickle of girls and women, but have simultaneously modeled the new and most profitable high-tech scientific enterprises as newly hip boys' clubs.

Patriarchy's fans in the political sphere, meanwhile, have not been able to prevent more women from running for elective office, but they have held them to standards of parenting and appearance that no male candidate has had to meet. Or they have accepted that more women will win seats in national legislatures, but then moved real decision-making power into the executive branch, especially into the secrecy-shrouded national security agencies. They have characterized "social safety net" policy areas—policy areas they used to control—as "soft" and thus "unmanly" and feminized, in order that these now-marginalized ministerial posts may be the ones awarded to newly ascendant political women.

Internationally, patriarchy's perpetuators have responded to the organizing of exploited women workers by moving their operations to neighboring countries whose patriarchal governments welcome them with open arms. They have accepted innovative gender advisors into their international agencies, but underfunded them and conveniently left them out of the decision-making loop. They have not been able to stop the passage of the historic UN Security Council Resolution 1325 on Women, Peace and Security, but they have gone about trying to shrink its actual implementation to simply adding more women to international military peacekeeping forces and acknowledging women as victims of wartime sexual assault, without increasing women's influence on peace agreements or post-peace reconstruction. They have promoted a handful of women to prominent international positions while intensely socializing them in the system's patriarchal norms so that they are less likely to rock the masculinity-privileging boat.

In local, national, and international arenas, patriarchy's diverse beneficiaries have portrayed the contemporary world as fraught with imminent dangers. To meet those alleged dangers—from amorphous terrorism, from global waves of immigrants fleeing wars, oppression, and natural disasters—patriarchy's contemporary modernizers propose hyper-militarization. The fact that militarizing modernization equips local police forces with heavy weaponry and gives license to border officials to turn back immigrants on the flimsiest of grounds makes the defense establishment the center of a government's foreign policy. Each of these moves depends on masculinization—of police, of border officials, of national security decision-making. That multi-stranded contemporary masculinization depends—as masculinization always does—on multiple processes of feminization. Victimized immigrant men must be feminized (while also being portrayed as threats). Community policing that engages in building trust through daily interactions with local citizens must be feminized, even if the majority of the officers doing this work are men. Diplomats and entire ministries of foreign affairs must be portrayed as relatively unmanly.

Through old means and new, patriarchy's beneficiaries hold out enticing carrots that have caused many of the people who do not share in its chief rewards to be complicit in its perpetuation. Recognizing patriarchy's old and updated allures is one of the first steps toward challenging this perpetuation.

Patriarchal complicity is not the same as patriarchal power. Patriarchal complicity can be engaged in by women, men, and transgender people. It can be engaged in by people who think of themselves as living far from the centers of privilege. Patriarchal complicity can take the form, for instance, of gaining emotional solace when vicariously grieving as one walks across a now-serene battlefield. It can lure one into being satisfied with—even proud of—only one side's narrative of a past conflict. Patriarchal complicity can boost one's self-esteem when accepting a promotion over other talented women and racially marginalized people. Such complicity can generate personal excitement at being associated with the winning team, company, party, or nation, without delving too deeply into the formula for that group's success. Patriarchal complicity can take the form of being reassured in one's own personal security when accepting the legitimacy of new exclusionary laws and practices.

The fodder for patriarchal complicity is inattentiveness and lack of a feminist curiosity.

One is likely to slide into such complicity if one imagines that one's own condition is representative of others' conditions. Paying serious attention to—seeking out, listening carefully to, becoming informed about—the daily experiences of women and men and transgender people in other ethnic, racial, class, sexual, religious, and national groups can guard against becoming complicit in the perpetuation of patriarchy. This attentiveness can be practiced in one's own family, in one's own workplace. The dismissive raised eyebrow, the flick of the skirt, the scornful smirk—being attentive requires watching for the unspoken, rarely recorded gestures that serve to perpetuate the sexist norm. Resisting the minute gestures that serve to sustain patriarchy requires not just recording them but naming them, speaking out against them.

This noticing can be hard to do. It proves hardest when one is left isolated in noting it and challenging it. Reversing inattentiveness is most effective when the one person who names out loud the patriarchal smirk is backed up by someone else who may not have noticed that smirk but now realizes its significance.

A lack of feminist curiosity is closely aligned with inattentiveness. Sustaining patriarchy relies on most people being lazy. Patriarchy is most easily perpetuated when most people take what is happening—the familiar and the new—as unproblematic and thus unworthy of being seriously investigated. More manly SUVs on the road? Oh, that's just the market at work. More middle-class households hiring nannies so that the adult woman can hold down a full-time paying job? That's just social change. More and more clothes and electronic devices being assembled in factories overseas? That's just the workings of profit-maximizing capitalism, and has nothing to do with the cheapening of women's labor. The rise of far-right nationalist political parties? Alarming, but it is only about racism, requiring no feminist-informed investigation.

Furthermore, those extremist movements only underscore the rationality of the center's male establishment. Today, and in any current moment, there may arise a particularly virulent or blatant form of patriarchy—a blustering misogynist leader, an extreme form of fundamentalism, an outrageously xenophobic political party. Each of these catches our attention. Each of these allows us to express vocal dismay. Insofar as all of these manifestations of patriarchy are abusive and retrograde, they certainly deserve attention and condemnation. These, however, are not the chief engines of sustainable patriarchy. Together, they make ordinary updated patriarchy look tame, and thus unworthy of serious resistance. Perhaps even more helpful to the beneficiaries of patriarchy, when we are prioritizing the most outrageous (and photogenic) forms of today's patriarchy, we slip into imagining that the ordinary patriarchs are the "rational men" who will protect us and do all the serious thinking on our behalf.

The antidote to a patriarchally complicit lack of curiosity is asking new feminist-informed questions. Lots of questions. Conducting deep and ongoing feminist investigations of the institutions apparently at the forefront of modern life is a crucial form of resistance. It is dismaying how little we all know about how patriarchal beliefs, values, and relationships shape the operations of the Bank of England, the New York Stock Exchange, Hilton Hotels, Microsoft, Facebook, Shell Oil, Samsung, NATO, the Chinese Communist Party's Politboro, the Russian Orthodox Church, the BBC, 21st Century Fox, the Ministry of Defense, the Pentagon, the US National Security Council. Every one of these organizations can be investigated. None of them should be immune to feminist curiosity.

Yes, each of these investigations will take a collective effort of feminist-informed investigators with diverse skills. Still, it is possible. Just because an organization wields exceptional influence does not mean it is off-limits for curious feminists. Just because an institution exercises vast power does not mean it is ungendered.

Stopping in their tracks the efforts to sustain patriarchy needs organized, cross-race, inter-generational, transnational resistance. Yet that mobilization—energizing at the most local level but infused with a global consciousness—needs to be coupled with fresh thinking. One of the elements of past and current feminist activism that has been crucial to tilting and shredding patriarchy has been crafting new feminist concepts. When it works, a concept enables us to see past the allegedly new, to see what gendered unfairness and inequities are being perpetuated, and gives us a language to speak about them with one another. Here are just some of the concepts that have proved illuminating:

- women's suffrage
- women's rights
- equal pay
- comparable worth
- domestic violence
- reproductive rights
- militarized masculinities
- date rape
- sexual harassment
- the glass ceiling
- everyday sexism
- systematic wartime rape
- gender-based violence

Any useful fresh feminist concept should make even the most alluring operations of updated patriarchy newly transparent for what they are. And patriarchy made transparent is patriarchy made vulnerable.

Paying feminist attention, asking feminist questions, conducting feminist investigations, crafting gender-revealing concepts, creating diversely welcoming broad alliances, and acting with care and creativity—patriarchy doesn't stand a chance.

NOTES

CHAPTER 1. PINK PUSSY HATS VS. PATRIARCHY

1. "Nova Scotia Hosts One of the Smallest Women's Marches, But Still It's Mighty," Canadian Broadcasting Corporation, www.cbc.ca /news/canada/nova-scotia/women-s-march-on-washington-sandy-cove-digby-neck-donald-trump-1.2899568, accessed January 24, 2017.

2. Two American professors, Jeremy Pressman (University of Connecticut) and Erica Chenoweth (University of Denver) and a team of their students drew on local official, press, first-hand-witness, and photographic evidence to arrive at preliminary estimates of the numbers of people who participated in the January 21, 2017 Women's Marches in towns and cities across the United States and around the world. In an effort to make their estimates as reliable as possible, Pressman and Chenoweth offer for each march a high and a low figure. Thus the high figure for the Toronto march is 60,000, while the low estimate is 50,000. Jeremy Pressman and Erica Chenoweth, "Crowd Estimates, 1.21.2017," January 25, 2017, https://docs.google.com/spreadsheets/d /1xaoiLqYKz8x9Yc_rfhtmSOJQ2EGgeUVjvV4A8LsIaxY/htmlview?sle =true#grid=0, accessed January 25, 2017.

3. Pressman and Chenoweth, op. cit.

4. Meredith Woerner, "Who started the march? One Woman," *Los Angeles Times*, January 21, 2017, http://latimes.com/nation/la-na-pol-womens-march-live-who-started-the-march-one-1485033621-htmlstory.html.

5. "2016 Election Analysis: Women Voters Did Not Abandon Clinton: Nor Did She Fail to Win Their Support," Barbara Lee Family Foundation and Center for American Women and Politics (CAWP), Rutgers University, November 11, 2016, http://cawp.rutgers.edu/sites/default/files/resources/pgw_press_release_nov_11_women_voters_final.pdf, accessed February 19, 2017. The Rutgers-based Center for American Women and Politics is one of the most authoritative sources for data on and analysis of US gendered patterns of voting and office-holding at both state and federal level. CAWP's researchers regularly investigate racial patterns within gendered patterns, thus reporting on women of color both as voters and as public office-holders.

6. "Behind Trump's victory: Divisions by race, gender and education," Pew Research Center, www.pewresearch.org/fact-tank/2016/11/09/behind-trumps-victory, accessed November 13, 2016. CAWP, "2016 Election Analysis," op. cit.

7. From November 2016 to January 2017, the American organizing group for the Women's March became a racially and culturally diverse group of about fourteen young women. When, ten days before the march, *Vogue* magazine invited the organizers to come to a studio for a collective photo, the following women arrived: Ting Ting Cheng, Tabitha St. Bernard, Janaye Ingram, Paola Mendoza, Cassady Fendlay, Linda Sarsour, Bob Bland, Nantasha Williams, Breanne Butler, Ginny Suss, Sarah Sophie Flicker, Tamika Mallory, Carmen Perez, Vanessa Wruble. Most had not known each other before November. Many had never organized a demonstration. Julia Felsenthal, "These Are the Women Organizing the Women's March on Washington," *Vogue*, January 10, 2017, www.vogue.com/13520360/meet-the-women-of-the-womens-march-on-washington, accessed January 27, 2017.

8. Pressman and Chenoweth, "Crowd Estimates," op. cit.

9. Women's March on Washington: Sister Marches, www.womensmarch.com/sisters, accessed February 1, 2017.

10. Pressman and Chenoweth, "Crowd Estimates," op. cit.

11. Ibid.

12. See www.womensmarch.com, accessed January 15, 2017.

13. Seema Mehta, "How these Los Angeles-born pink hats became a worldwide symbol of the anti-Trump women's march," *Los Angeles Times*, January 15, 2017: www.latimes.com/politics/la-pol-ca-pink-hats-womens-march-20170115-story.html, accessed January 30, 2017.

14. Joshua Lott, Getty Images, published in the *Boston Globe*, January 29, 2017. Signs quoted from the Washington Women's March are from the author's own photographs, Washington, DC, January 21, 2017.

15. Alexandra Alter, "Fears for the Future Prompt a Boon for Dystopian Classics," *New York Times*, January 28, 2017. Alter also reports that sales of Margaret Atwood's *The Handmaid's Tale* increased by 30 percent in 2016 over those in 2015.

16. Chinese feminist translator at the Washington Women's March, interviewed afterward by the author, February 18, 2017. Because of the political sensitivity of this activism, the interviewee asked to remain anonymous.

17. Author's conversation with a Chinese feminist reporter of the Washington Women's March, February 17, 2017. Because of the sensitivity of her role, she must remain anonymous.

18. Email correspondence by the author with Lepa Mladjenović, January 25, 2017.

19. Email correspondence by the author with Ailbhe Smyth, January 22, 2017.

20. Email correspondence by the author with Elin Liss, January 24, 2017.

21. Somini Sengupta, "Margot Wallström on Feminism, Trump and Sweden's Future," *New York Times*, December 18, 2016.

22. Stockholm International Peace Research Institute, one of the premier collectors and analysts of worldwide arms manufacture, imports and exports: www.sipri.org, accessed February 1, 2017.

23. Email correspondence by the author with Elin Liss, January 24, 2017.

24. Among the most influential feminist writers spelling out these gendered sources of war and militarism has been the British author/researcher Cynthia Cockburn. See, for instance: Cynthia Cockburn, *From Where We Stand: War, Women's Activism and Feminist Analysis*

(London and New York: Zed Books, 2007); Cynthia Cockburn, *Anti-Militarism* (London and New York: Palgrave Macmillan, 2012). Also consistently insightful about the reinforcing interplay of nationalism and militarism have been the analyses offered by transnational women's rights organizations: the Women's International League for Peace and Freedom: www.wilpf.org, and Women Living Under Muslim Laws: www.wluml.org.

25. Peter Kellner, "Brexit: Why Nobody Can Predict How the U.K. Will Vote," *Newsweek*, June 20, 2016, www.newsweek.com/final-week-brexit-safety-first-471153, accessed January 31, 2016; "EU Referendum: Full Results and Analysis," *The Guardian*, June 24, 2016, www.theguardian.com/politics/ng-interactive/2016/jun/23/eu-referendum-live-results-and-analysis, accessed June 24, 2016; Peter Kellner, "General Election 2015: how Britain really voted," *Prospect*, June 4, 2015, www.prospectmagazine.co.uk/blogs/peter-kellner/general-election-2015-how-britain-really-voted, accessed July 1, 2015.

26. Charlotte Proudman and Mary Honeyball, "Six big reasons for women to vote Remain in the EU referendum," *The Independent*, June 23, 2016, www.independent.co.uk/voices/eu-referendum-brexit-nigel-farage-david-cameron-women-reasons-vote-remain-a7097271.html, accessed January 31, 2017.

27. "The Gender Pay Gap," London, The Fawcett Society, 2016: www.fawcettsociety.org.uk/policy-research/the-gender-pay-gap, accessed February 1, 2017.

28. "Ethnic Minorities in Politics and Public Life," London, House of Commons Library, March 4, 2016: http://researchbriefings.files.parliament.uk/documents/SN01156/SN01156.pdf, accessed February 1, 2017.

29. "Fawcett Launches Sex Discrimination Law Review," London, Fawcett Society, January 30, 2017: www.fawcettsociety.org.uk/2017/01/sex-discrimination-law, accessed February 1, 2017.

30. British feminist Laura Bates is the founder of the Everyday Sexism Project, whose website invites women to record their own experiences of everyday sexism: www.everydaysexism.com.

31. Margot Lee Shetterly, *Hidden Figures* (New York: William Morrow, 2016).

32. One of the most nuanced feminist-informed investigations of a masculinized authoritarian ruler—and local feminists' responses—is: Valerie Sperling, *Sex, Politics and Putin* (Oxford: OUP, 2015).

33. *The Wilmar 8* is a filmed documentary (1981), directed by Lee Grant, recounting the strike by eight women working in a branch bank in the small town of Wilmar, Minnesota, who became fed up after training men and then seeing them promoted while they remained stuck in the low-paid tellers' jobs. The women lost their fight.

34. Inter-Parliamentary Union, www.ipu.org/wmn-e/world.htm, accessed February 4, 2017.

CHAPTER 4. TICERONDA, GETTYSBURG, AND HIROSHIMA

1. See www.fortticonderoga.org.

2. See www.nps.gov/gett; and www.historynet.com.

3. Drew Gilpin Faust, *This Republic of Suffering: Death and the American Civil War* (New York: Knopf, 2008).

4. Cynthia Enloe, *Globalization and Militarism: Feminists Make the Link* (Lanham, MD: Rowman and Littlefield, 2nd edition, 2016).

5. N.A. Taylor and Robert Jacobs, eds., "Re-imagining Hiroshima," special issue, *Critical Military Studies* 1.2 (2015).

6. See http://hpmmuseum.jp.

7. Rick Rojas, "Seventy Years on, Crowd Gets as Close It Can to the Birthplace of the Bomb," *New York Times*, April 6, 2015; Nathan Hodge and Sharon Weinberger, *A Nuclear Family Vacation: Travels in the World of Atomic Weaponry* (New York: Bloomsbury, 2008).

8. Katie Engelhart, "When the Bombs Rained Down," *New York Times*, August 30, 2015.

CHAPTER 5. PATRIARCHAL FORGETTING AT GALLIPOLI, THE SOMME, AND THE HAGUE

Some of the feminist works that have influenced me in writing this essay:

Acton, Carol, *Grief in Wartime* (New York: Palgrave, 2007).

Altınay, Ayşe Gül, *The Myth of the Military-Nation* (New York: Palgrave, 2004).

Altınay, Ayşe Gül and Andrea Pétő, editors, *Gendered Wars, Gendered Memories* (London and New York: Routledge, 2016).

Brittain, Vera, *Testament of Youth* (London: Virago, 1978).

Badran, Margot, *Feminists, Islam, and Nation: Gender and the Making of Modern Egypt* (Princeton: Princeton University Press, 1995).

Carden-Coyne, Ana, *Reconstructing the Body: Classicism, Modernism, and the First World War* (Oxford and New York: Oxford University Press, 2009).

Carden-Coyne, Ana, ed., *Gender and Conflict since 1914* (London: Palgrave Macmillan, 2012).

Confortini, Catia Cecilia, *Intelligent Compassion: Feminist Critical Methodology in the Women's International League for Peace and Freedom* (Oxford and New York: Oxford University Press, 2012).

Grace, Patricia, *Tu: A Novel* (Auckland, New Zealand: Penguin Books, 2004).

Grazel, Susan R., *Women's Identities at War* (Chapel Hill: University of North Carolina Press, 1999).

Levenback, Karen L., *Virginia Woolf and the Great War* (Syracuse: Syracuse University Press, 1999).

Levine, Philippa, *Prostitution, Race and Politics: Policing Venereal Disease in the British Empire* (London and New York: Routledge, 2003).

"Talking with Our Grandmothers: World War I and the Women's Peace Movement": http://ww1womenspeacemovement.com/node/5.

Winslow, Barbara, *Sylvia Pankhurst* (London: UCL Press, 1996).

Woolf, Virginia, "A Society," (first published in 1921), republished in *The Lady in The Looking Glass* (London and New York: Penguin, 2011, pp.11–34).

CHAPTER 6. A FLICK OF THE SKIRT

In thinking through the implications of this study, I have greatly benefited from conversations with Jef Huymans.

I also would like to personally thank Maya Eichler, Teresia Teaiwa, Vron Ware, Alex Hyde, Martha Ackelsberg, David Vine, Aakriti Pandey, Nicola Lester, and Tom Gregory for sharing sources and ideas that have enriched this article.

1. I was introduced to the ideas of Egyptian feminist Huda Al Sha'arawi by Margot Badran, in her eye-opening book *Feminists, Islam and the Nation: Gender and the Making of Modern Egypt* (Princeton: Princeton University Press, 1995).

2. Mary Wollstonecraft, *A Vindication of the Rights of Woman*, ed. Miriam Brody Kramnick (revised edition, London: Penguin, 2004).

3. Cynthis Enloe, *Bananas, Beaches and Bases*, updated 2nd edition (Berkeley and London: University of California Press, 2014). Philippa Levine, *Prostitution, Race and Politics: Policing Venereal Disease in the British Empire* (London and New York: Routledge, 2003). Judith Walkowitz, *Prostitution and Victorian Society* (Cambridge and New York: Cambridge University Press, 1980).

4. Ann D. Gordon, editor, *The Selected Papers of Elizabeth Cady Stanton and Susan B. Anthony*, Vol. 5 (New Brunswick, NJ: Rutgers University Press, 2009). Clare Midgley, *Women Against Slavery: The British Campaigns 1780–1870* (London and New York: Routledge, 1992).

5. Virginia Woolf, *Three Guineas* (New York: Harcourt Brace, 2006), pp.76–7.

6. Mahiye Seçil Dağtaş, "The Personal in the Collective: Rethinking the Secular Subject in Relation to the Military, Wifehood, and Islam in Turkey," pp.70–97, and Harriet Gray, "The Geopolitics of Intimacy and the Intimacies of Geopolitics: Combat Deployment, Post-Traumatic Stress Disorder, and Domestic Abuse in the British Military," pp.138–65, both in "Everyday Militarism," a special issue of *Feminist Studies*, vol. 42, No. 1, 2016. Maj Hedegaard Heiselberg, "Fighting for the Family," in "Becoming a Warring Nation: Adjusting to War and Violence in Denmark," special issue of *Critical Military Studies*, volume 3, issue 1, 2017.

7. Sarah Bulmer and Alexandra Hyde, "An Introduction to Encounters," *Military Critical Studies*, issue 1, vol. 1, 2015, p.79.

8. Svetlana Alexievich, *Zinky Boys: Soviet Voices from the Afghanistan War* (New York: Norton, 1992). Nicola Lester, "When a Soldier Dies," *Critical Military Studies*, vol. 1, issue 3, 2015, pp.249–53.

9. Denise Kiernan, *The Girls of Atomic City* (New York: Touchstone Books, 2013). Kate Brown, *Plutopia: Nuclear Families, Atomic Cities, and the Great Soviet and American Plutonium Disasters* (Oxford and New York: Oxford University Press, 2013). Hugh Gusterson, *Nuclear Rites: A Weapons*

Laboratory at the End of the Cold War (Berkeley: University of California Press, 1996).

10. Rosa Brooks, *How Everything Became War and the Military Became Everything: Tales from the Pentagon* (New York: Simon and Schuster, 2016).

11. Alexandra Hyde, *Inhabiting No-Man's-Land: The Military Mobilities of Army Wives*, PhD Dissertation, London, London School of Economics and Political Science, 2015.

12. Ibid., p.102

13. Matthew Green, "Military Wives Demand Action on Psychological Wounds of War," *The Guardian*, February 25, 2017, www.theguardian.com/uk-news/2017/feb/26/military-wives-ptsd-mental-health-speak-out-raise-awareness, accessed February 27, 2017. See also the BBC's audio documentary series, The Enemy Within, for additional interviews regarding British soldiers' and their wives' experiences of PTSD.

14. Ibid. Cynthia Enloe, *Nimo's War, Emma's War: Making Feminist Sense of the Iraq War* (Berkeley: University of California Press, 2010). Sarah Hautzinger and Jean Scandlyn, *Beyond Post-Traumatic Stress: Homefront Struggles with the Wars on Terror* (Walnut Creek, CA: Left Coast Press, 2014).

15. Teresia Teaiwa, in conversation with the author, Nadi, Fiji, July 5, 2015.

16. Vron Ware, *Military Migrants: Fighting for Your Country* (London: Palgrave, 2012).

17. Ibid.

18. David Vine, *Base Nation* (New York: Metropolitan Books, 2015).

19. Obi Anyadike, "A Rough Guide to Foreign Military Bases in Africa," *Irin News*, February 15, 2017, http://www.irinnews.org/feature/2017/02/15/rough-guide-foreign, accessed February 16, 2017. Andrew Jacobs and Jane Perlez, "U.S. Wary of a Chinese Base Rising as Its Neighbor in Africa," *New York Times*, February 26, 2017.

20. Sanne Terlingen and Hannah Kooy, "Fear and Loathing in Djibouti," *One World*, Netherlands, September 6, 2016: https://longreads.oneworld.nl/en/djibouti_data_traffic, accessed September 6, 2016.

21. David Vine, *Base Nation*, op. cit.

22. Martha Ackelsberg and Judith Plaskow, "Why We're Not Getting Married," *Lilith*, Fall 2004, www.lilith.org/articles/why-were-not-getting-married, accessed January 13, 2017.

CHAPTER 7. A WINDING ROAD TO FEMINIST CONSCIOUSNESS

1. Cynthia Enloe, *Does Khaki Become You? The Militarization of Women's Lives* (London: Pluto Press; Boston: South End Press, 1983).

2. My initial exploration into Gurkha history was: Cynthia H. Enloe, *Ethnic Soldiers: State Security in Divided Societies* (London: Penguin, 1980). Gurkha history hasn't come to a halt. For more on today's European male private security company employers' ethnicized and masculinized presumptions about Gurkha men, and about Gurkha men's own assessments of serving as employees of private security companies, see: Amanda Chisholm, "The Silenced and Indispensible: Gurkhas in Private Military Security Companies," *International Feminist Journal of Politics* 16.1 (2014), pp.26–47.

3. A Clark student, Seira Tamang, herself the daughter of a Gurkha, opened my eyes to the pressures imposed by British military officials on women such as her mother, a Gurkha wife. My first effort to think about the Nepalese women married to those Nepalese men who joined the British Army's Gurkha regiments was: Cynthia Enloe, *Maneuvers: The International Politics of Militarizing Women's Lives* (Berkeley: University of California Press, 2000).

4. Betty Friedan, *The Feminine Mystique* (New York: Norton, 1963).

5. For my analysis of the Bangladeshi garment factory tragedies and the protracted debates over accountability and labor rights that came in their wake, I relied on the dogged journalistic sleuthing of the *New York Times*'s Steven Greenhouse: Cynthia Enloe, *Bananas, Beaches and Bases: Making Feminist Sense of International Politics* (Berkeley: University of California Press, revised and updated 2nd ed., 2014). Among the recent investigative journalistic accounts that I have read, reread, underlined, and filed are: Sarah Maslin Nir, "The Price of Nice Nails," *New York Times*, May 7, 2015; Sarah Maslin Nir, "Perfect Nails, Poisoned Workers," *New York Times*, May 8, 2015.

6. Blanche Wiesen Cook, *Eleanor Roosevelt*, 3 vols (New York: Viking, 1992, 1999, 2016).

7. Hannah Arendt, *The Origins of Totalitarianism* (New York: Harcourt Brace, 1951).

8. Donna Kate Rushin, "The Bridge Poem," *This Bridge Called My Back*, ed. Cherrie Moraga and Gloria Anzaldua (Watertown, MA: Persephone Books, 1981), pp.xxi–xxii. Gloria T. Hull, Patricia Bell-Scott, and Barbara Smith, eds., *But Some of Us Are Brave* (Old Westbury, NY: Feminist Press, 1982). The full title given to this ground-breaking Black feminist collection by Hull, Scott and Smith was: "All of the Women are White, All the Blacks are Men, But Some of Us Are Brave."

9. Ximena Bunster, "Surviving Without Fear: Women and Torture in Latin America," *Women and Change in Latin America*, eds. June Nash and Helen Safa (South Hadley, MA: Bergin and Garvey, 1986), pp.297–326.

10. Kathleen Barry, *Female Sexual Slavery* (New York: Avon, 1979); and Susan Brownmiller, *Against Our Will* (Boston: Beacon Books, 1975).

11. Myna Trustram, *Women of the Regiment: Marriage and the Victorian Army* (Cambridge, MA: Cambridge University Press, 1984); Judith Walkowitz, *Prostitution and the Victorian Society* (Cambridge, UK: Cambridge University Press, 1980).

12. Philippa Levine, "'Walking the Streets in a Way No Decent Woman Should': Women Police in World War One," *Journal of Modern History* 66 (1994), pp.34–78; Philippa Levine, "Battle Colors: Race, Sex and Colonial Soldiery in World War I," *Journal of Women's History* 9.4 (1998), pp.104–30; Philippa Levine, *Prostitution, Race and Politics: Policing Venereal Disease in the British Empire* (London and New York: Routledge, 2003).

13. Joni Seager and Ann Olson, *Women in the World: An International Atlas* (New York: Simon and Schuster, 1986). A new, updated 5th edition of Seager's Women's Atlas will be published by Myriad Editions in 2018.

14. The most recent, updated edition of this remarkable atlas is: Joni Seager, *The Penguin Atlas of Women in the World*, 4th ed. (New York: Penguin, 2009).

15. J. Ann Tickner, *Gender in International Relations* (New York: Columbia University Press, 1992); J. Ann Tickner, *A Feminist Voyage*

Through International Relations (Oxford and New York: Oxford University Press, 2014).

16. "Five Key Points for a Differential Treatment of Sexual Violence in the Accords on Transitional Justice in the Peace Process," No Time to Keep Quiet Campaign, Sisma Mujer Corporation, National Network of Women, and Humanas Corporation. Bogotá, Colombia, April 27, 2015, www.sismamujer.org/wp-content/uploads/2016/04/Cinco-Subclaves-Reparacion.pdf.

CHAPTER 8. CAFETERIA LADIES, WONDER WOMAN AT THE UN, AND OTHER ACTS OF RESISTANCE

1. "Equal Pay Day," The Fawcett Society, November 10, 2016, www.fawcettsociety.org.uk/our-work/campaigns/equal-pay-day, accessed February 19, 2017.

2. "Global Gender Gap Report 2016," http://reports.weforum.org/?global-gender-gap-report-2016.

3. These and the rankings below come from the Global Gender Gap Report 2016, op. cit.

4. An engrossing feminist exploration of contemporary London's neighborhoods, each with its own distinctive gendered connections to the world's war zones and international migrations, is Cynthia Cockburn, *Looking to London: Women's Tales of War, Refuge and Re-homing* (London: Pluto Press, 2017).

5. Town Charts, Everett MA Demographics: www.towncharts.com/Massachusetts/Demographics/Everett-city-MA-Demographics-data.html, accessed February 12, 2017.

6. AreaVibes, based on 2015 data from the US Census Bureau: www.areavibes.com/everett-ma/employment, accessed February 12, 2017.

7. Town Charts, op. cit.

8. This account is drawn principally from: Shirley Leung, "A triumph long in coming in fair pay fight," *Boston Globe*, August 3, 2016.

9. Both Jancsy and Simonelli quoted in Leung, "A triumph long in coming in fair pay fight," op. cit.

10. Germaine Greer and Beatrix Campbell, "Tea and Militancy," *The Guardian*, October 2, 2010, www.theguardian.com/world/2010/oct

/02/made-in-dagenham-a-feminist-view, accessed February 14, 2017. See also: "Beatrix Campbell & the 'Dagenham' Moment," *History Workshop*, October 14, 2010, www.historyworkshop.org.uk/beatrix -campbell-dagenham, accessed February 14, 2017; Simon Goodley, "Dagenham Sewing Machinists Recall Strike That Changed Women's Lives," *The Guardian*, June 6, 2013, www.theguardian.com/politics/2013 /jun/06/dagenham-sewing-machinists-strike, accessed February 14, 2017. Today, a British feminist group that keeps close tabs on the UK's continuing gender pay gap (13.9 percent in late 2016) is the Fawcett Society. See, for instance, its "Equal Pay Day," and "The Gender Pay Gap," 2016, www.fawcettsociety.org.uk, accessed February 19, 2017.

11. Beatrix Campbell, *Wigan Pier Revisited: Politics and Poverty in the 1980s* (London: Virago, 1984); Dana Frank, *Bananeras: Women Transforming the Banana Unions of Latin America* (Cambridge, MA: South End Press, 2005); Cynthia Enloe, *Bananas, Beaches and Bases* (Berkeley and London: University of California Press, revised edition 2014).

12. Stephanie Ebbert, "Jolted, Women Get Set to Run," *Boston Globe*, February 16, 2017.

13. Shirley Leung, "The Equalizers: Patricia Jehlen and Ellen Story," *Boston Globe Magazine*, December 18, 2016, p.25. It should be noted that the *Boston Globe* journalist Shirley Leung played an important role in keeping before the local public's eye the story of the Everett lunch ladies' fight for equal pay.

14. This account draws on both of Shirley Leung's *Boston Globe* 2016 articles.

15. Stacy Cowley, "Pay Equity the Aim, Interviewers Can't Ask 'What Do You Make?'," *New York Times*, August 3, 2016.

16. Dorothy Simonelli, quoted in Shirley Leung, "A triumph long in coming in fair pay fight," *Boston Globe*, August 3, 2016.

17. Volume 3, the last volume in Blanche Wiesen Cook's definitive biography of Eleanor Roosevelt, includes a fascinating account of the efforts of "ER," starting while World War II still raged, to shape the nascent United Nations so that it would make anti-racism, anti-colonialism, human rights, and women's genuine participation its institutional centerpieces: Blanche Wiesen Cook, *Eleanor Roosevelt: The War Years and After, 1939–1962*, Volume 3, New York: Viking, 2016.

18. *UN Tribune*, www.untribune.com/where-do-the-41000-people-working-for-the-un-secretariat-come-from, accessed February 22, 2017.

19. UN Women, "Representation of Women in the United Nations Secretariat," November 2012, www.unwomen.org/en/how-we-work/un-system-coordination/women-in-the-united-nations, accessed February 22, 2017.

20. Karin Landgren, "The Lost Agenda: Gender Parity in Senior UN Appointments," *Global Peace Operations Review*, December 14, 2015, http://peaceoperationsreview.org/commentary/the-lost-agenda-gender-parity-in-senior-un-appointments, accessed October 8, 2016.

21. See, for instance, Dionne Searcey, Norimitsu Onishi, and Somini Sengupta, "Clinics for World's Vulnerable Brace for Trump's Anti-Abortion Cuts," *New York Times*, January 26, 2017.

22. Over the years, I have been tutored in the gendered workings of the UN, including the political debates swirling around CSW's annual March meetings, by many generous feminist activists within the transnational civil society movement, including Madeleine Rees, Nadine Peuchguirbal, Anne Marie Goetz, Maria Butler, Abigail Ruane, Ray Achison, Cynthia Rothschild, Charlotte Bunch, Vanessa Farr, Nela Porobić Isaković, Elin Liss, Sanam Anderlini, Carol Cohn, and Lena Ag.

23. Amnesty International, USA Section, "A Fact Sheet on CEDAW: Treaty for the Rights of Women," www.amnestyusa.org/sites/default/files/pdfs/cedaw_fact_sheet.pdf, accessed February 22, 2017; CNN, "U.S. Drops the Ball on Women's Rights," March 8, 2013, http://edition.cnn.com/2013/03/08/opinion/baldez-womens-equality-treaty, accessed February 22, 2017.

24. NGO Working Group on Women, Peace and Security, www.womenpeacesecurity.org, accessed February 22, 2017. One of the best sources for on-going news of 1325's impact—and the end-runs done around it—is WILPF's UN office website: www.peacewomen.org.

25. In 2016, for instance, thanks to years of effort by transnationally organized feminist environmentalists and the Network of Women Ministers of the Environment, the UN Environment Program authorized the first-ever Earth-wide assessment of the gender dynamics shaping all aspects the planet's environment, including climate change:

www.unep.org/ggeo. Feminist geographer Joni Seager was this report's lead author.

26. For a description of the campaign to make "gender-based violence" a criterion in the UN-negotiated Arms Trade Treaty, see: Cynthia Enloe, *Bananas, Beaches and Bases* (Berkeley and London: University of California Press, revised edition, 2014).

27. UN Women, "SDG 5: Achieve Gender Equality and Empower All Women and Girls," UN Women, 2015, www.unwomen.org/en /news/in-focus/women-and-the-sdgs/sdg-5-gender-equality, accessed February 24, 2017.

28. This account draws upon reporting by several keen UN watchers: Anne Marie Goetz, "Still No Country for Women? Double Standards in Choosing the Next UN Secretary-General," *50-50: Inclusive Democracy,* July 28, 2016, www.opendemocracy.net/5050/anne-marie-goetz/still-no-country-for-women-double-standards-choosing-next-UN-Secretary-General, accessed July 30, 2016; Charlotte Bunch, correspondence with the author, August 5, 2016; as well as Somini Sengupta, "Security Council Backs New Leader for U.N.," *New York Times,* October 6, 2016; Somini Sengupta, "Known for Nerve and Savvy, Next U.N. Leader Needs Both," *New York Times,* October 14, 2016; International Center for Research on Women, "Toward a More Feminist United Nations: A 100 Day Agenda for the New Secretary-General," ICRW, Washington, D.C., December, 2016, www.icrw.org /publications/toward-feminist-united-nations-100-day-agenda-new -secretary-general, accessed January 9, 2017.

29. The following account is based on both news coverage and interviews with several feminists who have long histories of work in and around the UN. Because of the sensitivity of the protests that this Wonder Woman choice set off, I have assured these interviewees that I will keep their identities confidential. If readers find this too-brief account at all intriguing, I urge them to conduct a more extensive investigation. There are many questions still unanswered about the patriarchal dynamics inside the UN—and resistances to it.

30. See www.thepetitionsite.com/741/288/432/reconsider-the-choice-of -honorary-ambassador, accessed October 22, 2016. Somini Sengupta, "Wonder Woman Faces Challenge at U.N.: A Recall Petition," *New York Times,* October 21, 2016.

31. See www.thepetitionsite.com/741/288/432/reconsider-the-choice-of -honorary-ambassador, accessed October 22, 2016.

32 A meticulous and fascinating account of the invention of Wonder Woman, her credited inventor and her now-revealed women contributors is: Jill Lepore, *The Secret History of Wonder Woman*, New York: Knopf, 2014.

33. Amid the UN controversy, Lynda Carter, the part-Mexican American actress who played Wonder Woman in the US 1970s television series, gave an interview in which she defended Wonder Woman as iconic—not American, but "Amazonian." Alex Williams, "Wonder Woman Grapples with Modern Foes: Critics," *New York Times*, December 25, 2016.

34. See www.thepetitionsite.com/741/288/432/reconsider-the-choice-of -honorary-ambassador, accessed October 22, 2016. For another blistering critique, see this essay by Sanam Naraghi-Anderlini, co-founder of the International Civil Action Society Network (ICAN) and one of the long-time feminist activists lobbying the UN to take women seriously in peace and security policies and operations: http://sister-hood.com/ sanam-naraghi-anderlini/wonder-woman-makes-real-women-wonder -un, accessed November 3, 2016.

35. Nicole Puglise, "Wonder Woman announced as UN Ambassador Amid Staff Protest," *The Guardian*, October 21, 2016, www.theguardian .com/books/2016/oct/21/wonder-woman-un-ambassador-staff-protest, accessed December 14, 2016.

36. Nurith Aizenman, "Wonder Woman's U.N. Job Comes to an End," National Public Radio, December 13, 2016, www.npr.org/sections /goatsandsoda/2016/12/13/504968772/wonder-womans-u-n-job-comes -to-an-end, accessed December 14, 2016. See also: Erin McCann, "U.N. Shuts Down Campaign Featuring Wonder Woman," *New York Times*, December 14, 2016.

INDEX

Index

Eliot, T.S., 95
Enloe, Abraham, 114
Enloe, Cortez, 114, 115–16
Enloe, Cynthia, 113–34; academic
    career, 123–6; at Berkeley,
    California, 121–3; at Connecticut
    College, 119–21; background
    113–17; childhood in Manhasset,
    117–19; published works, 50–2, 54,
    55, 124–5, 126, 129–32
Enloe, Harriett Goodridge *see*
    Goodridge, Harriett
equality: marriage equality, 111; of
    rights for married women, 94, *see
    also* gender pay gap
Equality Now, 43
Erdoğan, Recep Tayyip, 19, 20
Ethnic Soldiers (Enloe), 126, 129, 177
ethnicity: ethnic diversity in
    Everett, 138; in former Yugosla-
    via, 34–5; of military wives
    104–5; in Syria and Iran, 30–1
European Union (EU): banana
    politics and, 52; Brexit vote,
    13–15, 172; Britain and the gender
    pay gap, 136
Everett lunch ladies: gender pay
    gap, 137–41, 143
Everyday Sexism Project, 172

families: marriage and, 112;
    post-World War I, 86
fascism, 9–10
Fawcett Society, 14–15, 172
femininities: courses and programs
    on, 132; gender pay gap and, 136;
    in international politics, 61–2, 63;
    military tourism sites and, 75–6;
    patriarchal, 19, 22; post-World
    War I developments, 85, 86
feminist activism *see under different
    countries*
feminist concepts, 127, 142, 167

feminist curiosity, 125; international
    politics and, 61–3; lack of, 165–6
feminization: gender pay gap and,
    138–40; globalized patriarchy
    and, 53–4; international politics,
    55; sustainable patriarchy and,
    160; of work and politics 22–3
Fijian women as military wives,
    104–5
foreign policy: feminist (Sweden),
    10–11
Fort Ticonderoga, 64–7, 68, 74
France: overseas military bases, 108,
    109; Women's Marches (2017), 11
Franco-Prussian War, 83
Free Speech Movement (Berkeley,
    California), 122–3
French Indo-China War, 83
French Revolution, 123
Friedan, Betty: *The Feminine
    Mystique*, 117

Gall, Carlotta, 119
Gallipoli, Battle of, 75, 78–82
Gallipoli (film), 78, 79
Gandhi, Indira, 19
The Gang's All Here (film), 50
garments *see* clothing manufacture
Gbowee, Leymah, 18–19, 39
gender: Brexit campaign and, 13–14;
    child marriage and, 25–6;
    gendered nature of the Syrian
    conflict, 41–3; parenting at
    militarized tourist sites, 69
gender analysis: of international
    politics, 52–63
Gender in International Relations
    (Tickner), 132
gender pay gap, 135–44, 172, 179–81;
    in Britain 14, 136, 172; comparable
    worth, 141–2, 143–4; Everett
    lunch ladies, 137–41, 143; Global
    Gender Gap rankings, 135–6;

187

ABOUT THE AUTHOR

Cynthia Enloe is a feminist writer and teacher who brings together activism and research cross-nationally. She has investigated women in the global garment, sneaker, banking, and banana industries, domestic work, diplomacy, and militarism. She is the author of 14 books, and her work has been translated into French, German, Icelandic, Japanese, Korean, Portuguese, Spanish, Swedish, and Turkish. She has published in *Ms.* Magazine and the *Village Voice*, and appeared on National Public Radio, Al Jazeera, C-Span, and the BBC. A Research Professor at Clark University in Massachusetts, she has taught at universities in Guyana, Malaysia, the UK, Japan, and Canada. She has been awarded honorary doctorates by SOAS University of London and the University of Lund, as well as the Howard Zinn Award for Lifetime Achievement.

OTHER FEMINIST BOOKS BY CYNTHIA ENLOE